W9-BZO-728

Mario Vasilj

MEDJUGORJE

The School of Gospa

VISIONARIES TESTIFY

Medjugorje, 2014

Published by:

Print Team Mostar

For Publisher:

Blago Vukoja

Editor:

Mario Vasilj

Translation by:

Andrijana Šego

Reviewers:

Fr. Stanko Dodig, Josip Lončar, Marko Tokić

Photos by:

Foto „Đani",

family of Anita and Rudolf Baier,

the Ivanković – Mijatović family,

the Dragičević – Soldo family,

the Pavlović – Lunetti family,

the Ivanković – Elez family,

Fr. Petar Ljubičić,

Siniša Hančić,

Zoran Grizelj,

Stipe Ćavar,

the Vasilj family

Prepressed and Published by:

Print Team Mostar

CIP - Katalogizacija u publikaciji
Nacionalna i univerzitetska biblioteka
Bosne i Hercegovine, Sarajevo

27-312.47-587.6(497.6 Međugorje)(082)

MEDJUGORJE : The school of Gospa / [editor]
Mario Vasilj ; [translation by Andrijana Šego] ;
photos by Foto "Đani" ... [et al.]. - Mostar :
Print Team, 2014. - 120 str. : ilustr. ; 21 cm

Prijevod djela: Gospina škola.

ISBN 978-9958-1940-4-7
1. Vasilj, Mario
COBISS.BH-ID 19848710

Gospa of Medjugorje – the Queen of Peace, by Croatian artist Petar Jakelić (on display at Hotel Villa Regina).

Introduction

For three decades, since the 24th of June 1981, six trustworthy visionaries in Medjugorje have had daily apparitions of the Blessed Virgin Mary or 'Gospa' – as She is called by our people. The communist government's attempts to discredit these young people have all failed. Despite daily abuse, police interrogation, psychological and other types of torture, the visionaries were adamant in their statement that what they had experienced was not the fruit of their imagination, that they were not mentally unstable and that they were not under the influence of drugs. They fiercely claimed that they had a truthful encounter with Mother Mary who presented Herself as the Queen of Peace and that She wanted to deliver a message, through them, that mankind is at a turning point and that it is necessary to constantly pray and fight for peace. Gospa calls upon us to renew ourselves and our families. She wants us to be examples and, with Her help, She wants us to renew others.

During this whole time, Medjugorje withstood denials, complaints and boycott. As a matter of fact, Medjugorje has become a world renowned place of peace, prayer, conversion, fasting and penance. It is a sanctuary where millions of people come to every year. Those who seek God keep returning to this small place in Herzegovina, to an atmosphere of unusual calm and prayer, for spiritual renewal and to receive incentive to live a life of quality under God's direct guidance.

This book is a testimony of the six visionaries – Ivanka, Mirjana, Ivan, Jakov, Marija and Vicka. It is a portrayal of Gospa's apparitions to Fr. Karlo Lovrić, a testimony by Fr. Jozo Zovko (a priest who is familiar with the phenomenon of Medjugorje from the very beginning) as well as a testimony by Fr. Petar Ljubičić, who, when the time comes, shall reveal Gospa's secrets to the world. We hope that their words will be of use to those who wish to grow spiritually, to mature in wisdom and to achieve other Christian virtues. So be it!

The Editor

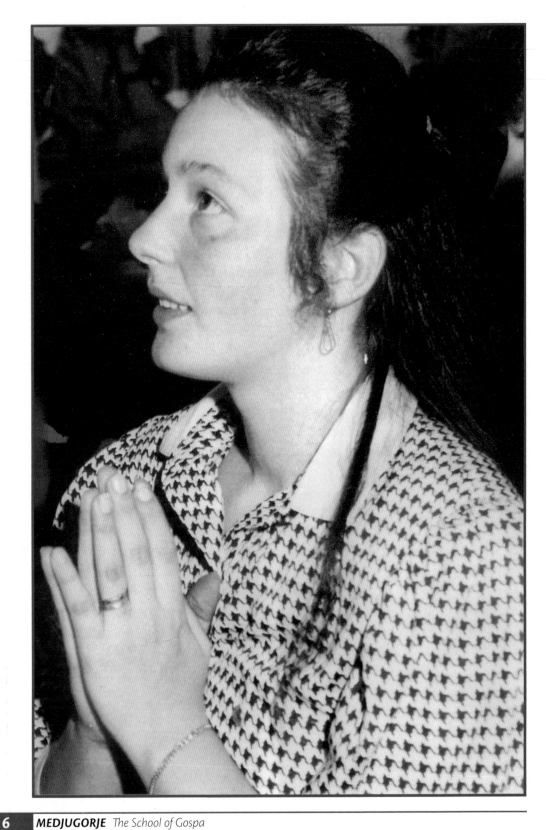

A Beautiful Woman with Kind and Warm Eyes
Ivanka Ivanković – Elez's Testimony

Ivanka Ivanković-Elez was born on the 21st of June 1966, in Bijakovići, Parish of Medjugorje. She was the first to see the Gospa. She had daily apparitions till the 7th of May 1985. On that day, upon receiving the tenth secret, Gospa told her that she would have one apparition once a year, on the 25th of June (the anniversary of the first apparition) for the rest of her life. Ivanka is married, has three children and lives with her family in Medjugorje. She prays for families.

PRAY WITH THE HEART!

First of all I would like to greet you with the most beautiful greeting of all: Praised be Jesus and Mary! To see Gospa with your own eyes is something really beautiful. However, to see Her with your eyes and not feel Her in your heart means nothing at all. Therefore, I have to say that I am an ordinary person just like the rest of you. God is as close to me as He is to you and my prayer is like your prayer. Despite this, for the last thirty years I have been asking myself the same questions: Lord, why me? Why did you give me this extraordinary gift and such a grave responsibility? However, I accept my mission without question and pray to God that He gives me the strength to go down the path that my Heavenly Mother shows me.

As your lives have their ups and downs, so does mine. However, already during the first apparition Gospa told us not to fear anything, that She will be with us forever as well as with those who believe in Her. Whenever we fall all we have to do is call Her and She shall come to lift us up. She also told us that we can stop any catastrophe such as war through prayer and by fasting. She has come to show us the way that leads to Her Son for He is not the one that has drifted away from us; it is us who have forgotten about Him. His love for us is so great that He shall never leave and abandon us. Therefore, our Mother constantly calls upon us and says, "Dear children, convert! Follow the path of peace, conversion, fasting and penance!"

In 1985, I was fifteen years old. Even though I was born and raised as a Christian, up to then I had never heard of Gospa appearing to anybody anywhere. During that year, my family was living in Mostar while Mirjana's family lived in Sarajevo. At the end of every school year we would always spend our vacation in Medjugorje. A simple walk on the 24th of June changed our lives as well as the lives of others. On that afternoon us girls agreed to meet on the outskirts of the village. Mirjana and I had arrived there first and we waited for our friends. I am not sure for how long we were waiting but I remember that we got tired of waiting and decided to return home.

On our way back, for no reason at all, I looked up towards the hill. That is when I saw Our Lady. I nudged Mirjana and said, "Look! Up there on the hill, it's Gospa!" She didn't turn to look. Instead, she uninterestingly replied, "Stop talking nonsense! What do you mean 'Gospa'!" I made up my mind to keep quiet and followed her home. When we arrived at the first houses, we came across Milka - Marija's sister. She was on her way to fetch the sheep from the field. She must have noticed the unusual expression on my face so she asked me, "Ivanka, what happened? Why do you look like that?" While I walked back with her I told her what I had just seen.

When we came close to the place where I saw Gospa, the two girls also saw what I saw. We felt mixed emotions. We cried, prayed and sang. In the meantime, Vicka came and noticed that there was something unusual going on. She asked us what was happening and we said, "Come here, we can see Gospa!" After disclosing this to her, she took her shoes off and ran away, toward the houses. On her way she met two boys, both named Ivan, and told them what the three of us had seen. Then three of them ran to us and joined us. They all saw what we had seen. Gospa was about six hundred meters away from us, motioning to come closer. Even though there were many of us, we did not dare go closer. We were afraid.

I don't remember how long we were there for. Some of us went home while the rest of us, full of tears and afraid, ran into the first house. We told the people in the house that we saw Gospa. I remember there were apples on the table and they took the apples and started throwing them at us, telling us that we were crazy and not to play with things like that. They told us to never repeat what we just said to anyone.

When I came home I told my grandmother, brother and sister what had happened. My brother and sister made fun of me and my grandmother said, "Child, that can't be. It must have been a shepherd you saw." That night was the longest night of my life. I was up all night wondering what was going on with me. Did I really see what I think I saw? Was I going crazy? What's the matter with me? Whoever we told what we saw, all of them said that it was impossible.

The next day the news of our encounter had travelled to the nearby villages. We all went back to that place. I remember my grandmother holding me by the hand. She said, "Whatever maybe up there, I don't care, you are not going." However, when the six of us saw a light on the hill flash three times, we climbed up the hill so fast that no one was able to keep up with us.

It is impossible to describe in words the beauty and love the woman we saw up there posses. Up to this day, I have never seen anything so beautiful: a young woman between nineteen and twenty-one years of age. She wore a grey dress, a white veil on Her head and a crown construed of stars. Her blue eyes were beautiful, warm and kind and She had black hair. She floated on a cloud. The inner peace, security and motherly love we felt can also not be described in words. At that moment I was positive that what was standing in front of us was Our Lady.

God granted me the mercy to speak to Her first. My mom had died just two months before the first apparition so I asked the Blessed Virgin Mary, "My Gospa, where is my mother?" She smiled at me and said that she was with Her. That is when She looked at all of us and said that we ought not be afraid for She would always be with us. That was exactly how it was, from the first day till now. If She were not with us this whole time, we surely would not be able to endure everything that followed.

This is where our Mother presented Herself as the Queen of Peace. Her first message to us was that of peace and then She invited us to pray, to convert, to fast and to repent. From the very first day, till today, these are the most important messages of Gospa of Medjugorje. These messages also contain the answers to the most important questions in life.

At the very start Gospa called upon us to pray seven Our Fathers, Hail Mary's, Glory Be's and the Credence every single day. She also asked that we pray all three parts of the Rosary and that we fast on bread and water twice a week. Our prayers have to come from the heart. The need to pray needs to be as air is for the lungs, as water is to the thirsty and as food is to the hungry, as man is not only a material being but also a spiritual one too.

I had apparitions every single day from 1981 to 1985. During these years Gospa spoke to me about Her life and about the future of the Church and the world. I wrote all this down. When She tells me to whom and when I must hand what I had written, I shall do so. The last regular apparition I had was on the 7th of May 1985. That was when Gospa entrusted me with the tenth secret. She told me that that was the last time I would be seeing Her on a daily basis and that I would be having apparitions once a year, on the 25th of June. On that day I received a great gift from Her. If any of you have ever wondered if there was life after death, as a living witness, I can testify that there really is. Our dear God granted me the grace to see my late mother as vividly as I see all of you now. My mother embraced me and said, "My child, I am so proud of you!"

From then on, every single day, I repeat that Gospa embraces all of us and says, "Dear children, do not fear! Follow the path of conversion, peace, fasting and penance." We are all people with the freedom to do what we please. She showed us the path we should follow in order not to wither and fail but we are free to decide which path we shall choose.

All six of us have our own mission. One prays for the youth, one for the ill, one for the priests and one for those who have not yet discovered God's loves. My mission is to pray for families. Gospa asks of us that we respect the Sacrament of Marriage, that we pray as a family once again, that we go to mass on Sundays, that we confess once a month and that the Bible becomes the centre of our family. If one wishes to turn a new leaf in life one first needs to make peace with him or herself and with his or her Creator. This can only be done during Holy Confession. Only upon doing so can we truly participate in the central event of Christian life, in Holy Mass, where the living Jesus comes to us. It is Him to whom we need to open our hearts to. If we truly believe in Him He will heal our pain and solve all our problems.

Gospa says that Satan is extremely strong and that he wishes to destroy our families. We can defend our family through prayer. Everything good comes from family: good priests, doctors, politicians... Therefore, if our family is healthy, the entire world shall be healthy. We often say that we do not have time for prayer, for our children and for family. This is not true. God has given us enough time for everything we just need to divide our time properly.

I pray for all families throughout the world every single day and I encourage you to do the same. I also wish to thank you for wanting to listen to Gospa's message and I thank you especially for wanting to accept Her with your heart and take Her back to your families, your parishes, fellow countrymen. I thank you also for wanting to be apostles of peace and for making examples of your own lives.

May our dear God and dear Gospa bless you and keep you safe on your journey and may you be blessed with peace in your hearts! Thank you!

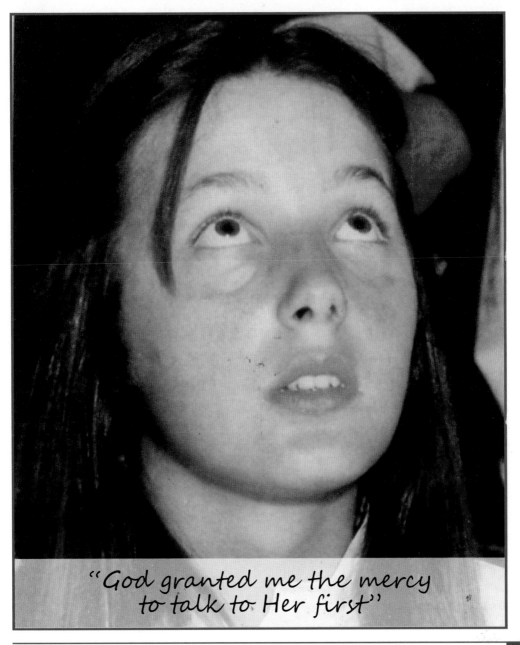

"God granted me the mercy to talk to Her first"

"Dear children!
The cross you built was part
of God's plan. During the
following days go to Cross Mountain
and pray beneath the cross.
I am in need of your prayers.
Thank you for
responding to my call!"

First Holy Mass held on Cross Mountain – March 1934

Pray The Credence

7 Our Fathers,
7 Hail Mary's and
7 Glory Be's
every single day

Reminder of the first Holy Mass on Cross Mountain
March 1934

To Learn of the Love of God
Mirjana Dragićević-Soldo's Testimony

Mirjana Dragićević-Soldo was born on the 18th of March 1965, in Sarajevo. She had daily apparitions from the 24th of June 1981 till the 25th of December 1982. On that day, after entrusting her with the tenth secret, Gospa told her that she would continue to have apparitions throughout her life, but only once a year – on the 18th of March. According to her, since the 2nd of August 1987, she hears the voice of Gospa on the 2nd of every month. During this occasion, she prays for non-believers with Her. Sometimes She also sees Her. Mirjana is married and has two children. She and her family live in Medjugorje. Her prayer intent entrusted to her by Gospa is to pray for non-believers; for those who have not yet come to know of the love of God.

ALLOW ANGLES TO SING IN YOUR HEARTS!

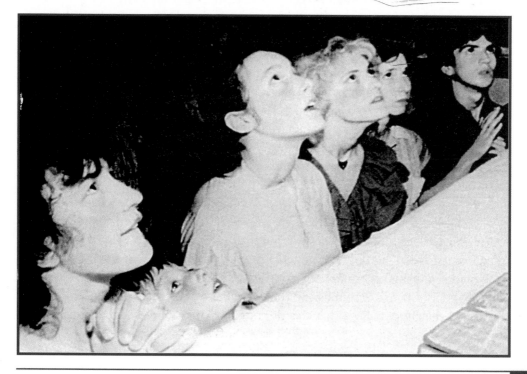

I greet you all with our traditional greeting: Praised be Jesus and Mary! I am happy that you have gathered in such number to celebrate Gospa and help Her realize Her plan concerning Medjugorje. This is a very special day for me. Those who have attended this morning's apparition know that our Mother was with us, that She blessed us with Her motherly love and left us another message, warning us how we should live if we wish to accept Her Son and give Him a deserving place. This is Gospa's message from this morning:

"Dear children, I have come with arms wide open, to embrace all of you and place you under my cloak. I cannot do this if your hearts are filled with false brightness and false idols. Purify your hearts and allow angels to sing in them. I will then cover you with my cloak and give Jesus to you and truly bring joy into your hearts. Do not wait my children! Thank you."

Gospa said, "Allow my angels to sing in your hearts." I too implore you to do so. Open your hearts and accept the love She wishes to give you. It is my personal belief that whoever comes to Medjugorje comes because She calls for them to come and because She is in need of each and everyone of us. Therefore, I will try to say what I deem very important, something I want you to keep in your hearts and take back home to your families.

As you may know, I had daily apparitions from the 24th of June 1981, till Christmas of 1982. This is when I received the tenth secret and when Gospa told me that She would not be appearing to me every single day anymore but that I shall have an apparition once a year, on the 18th of March, for the rest of my life. She also told me that I would have other apparitions too. These apparitions started on the 2nd of August, 1987, and they carry on to this day. I do not know until when I will have these latter apparitions. These apparitions occur on the 2nd of every month and the purpose of these apparitions is to pray for non-believers. Honestly, Gospa never used the word 'non-believer' because She says that by using it we are judging. Therefore, our Mother says, "for those who have not yet come to know of the love of God." She asks that we first pray for those who do not believe because most of what is bad such as wars, divorces, abuse of drugs and abortion come from them.

Gospa also says, "Dear children, whenever you pray for others you pray for yourselves, for your future." Besides wishing that we pray, She also wishes that we lead true Christian lives. This does not however mean that we should go around preaching, criticizing or judging others. On the contrary, it means that we should be examples of how God, His love, is within us and that we differ from "the children of this world". On the other hand, I believe that this does not mean that we need to keep quiet. I believe that Gospa wishes us to pray humbly and sincerely before we say anything.

If we pray, Jesus will talk through us. If we preach without praying first, what we say will have no meaning and we will be doing the opposite of what we are supposed to.

Gospa seeks that prayer for non-believers comes first, before all our other prayers. When I once asked Her who the non-believers were, She said, "All those who do not consider the Church as their home and God as their Father." Once during an apparition in Medjugorje the church was full of pilgrims. We were all praying and singing. The six of us childishly asked Gospa if She was happy because so many people were praying and celebrating Jesus. She looked at us with sad eyes and replied, "The number of fingers you have on your hands is the number of people praying in the church." This is exactly what Gospa wishes to convey to us: all those who do not feel that the Church is their home and that God is their Father - all are non-believers. I asked Her how we should pray for them, what the best way is and what prayer is the most affective. She replied, "My children, pray with your hearts. Every prayer from the heart is a good prayer. Feel the love for them in your hearts first. Think of them as your brothers and sisters who were not as fortunate as you have been to learn of the love of God. When you feel this for them, this is when you can pray for them. Do not criticize or judge them. Love them, pray for them and make examples of yourselves on how to live. This is how you shall change them. This is how you shall help them and this is how you shall wipe the tears that roll down my face for them."

As a mother, Gospa wishes that all Her children are on the right path, on the path that leads to Jesus Christ. She therefore suffers extremely when She sees Her children stray. This is why I encourage you, with all my heart, to pray for those who have not yet learned of the love of God. If only once could you see the tears Gospa sheds for the children who have strayed, I am sure you would pray for them with all your heart. Each six of us have received a special mission from Gospa. As I have already stated, mine is to pray for those that have not yet learned of the love of God. Vicka and Jakov pray for the ill, Ivan prays for the youth and priests, Marija prays for the souls in purgatory and Ivanka prays for families. Gospa constantly keeps reminding us that Holy Mass is the centre of Christian life. She once told us during an apparition while we were still children, "Dear children, if you need to choose between Holy Mass and an apparition, always choose Holy Mass, for my Son is with you then."

Never in all these years did Gospa ever say, "Pray and I shall answer your prayers." No, She always says, "Pray so that I may come to my Son with your prayers." Jesus has always been first. Many pilgrims believe that the seers are privileged and that all that they need to do is merely tell us their needs and that Gospa will answer their prayers. Some even think that by merely touching us their wishes will be granted. This is wrong thinking because all children are the same to our Mother, not one of us is privileged.

We are all Her children and She chooses each of us for various missions. She chose the six of us to convey Her messages and She chose all of you to be the apostles of those messages. In my opinion, a message from Her to the pilgrims testifies to this. The message said, "Dear children, I invited you, open your hearts, let me in so that I may make apostles of you."

This means that we all are chosen for a mission. However, if we must talk about privileges, then the messages in which Gospa mentions the priests let us conclude that they are the privileged ones. In these messages She never spoke of what they need to do but what we need to do for them. I have visited many other countries besides Bosnia and Herzegovina and Croatia and I have had a chance to see how these priests are treated in their countries. In comparison, they are treated very differently than our priests are treated by believers in Medjugorje. Our people still have respect for priests and this kind of respect is lacked in other countries. This is wrong and should not be happening. That is why Gospa says, "Dear children, if you loose your respect for priests you will also loose respect for the Church and, ultimately, for our dear God. If you believe that your priest is not as he is supposed to be, do not spread it to others for you are harming yourself and your listeners. Take the rosary and pray to God for him, fast for him and that is how you shall help him." Every time I especially tell pilgrims to set an example of how a priest should be treated and respected once they return to their parishes.

Our Heavenly Mother also wants us to reintroduce prayer into our families for nothing else can unite a family as prayer can. Parents have a responsibility to plant the seed of faith in their children's hearts. This is done best through prayer and by attending Holy Mass with your children. It is common knowledge that children learn best through examples; they imitate their parents and do what they do. Both parents should show their children that God and Gospa come first, before anything else in life.

I had the opportunity to talk with many young couples who visit Medjugorje from all over the world and they all say the same thing, "We do not have much time for prayer, we work a lot. We do not want our children to suffer the way we suffered. We want to leave them as much as we can once we are gone." Listening to them thinking this way, I feel great sadness and I think how their view on life is completely wrong. One can leave their children all the material wealth of this world, thousands and thousands of Euros but their children will never be satisfied and they will always want more. However, if parents show their children the need for Jesus and teach them that He comes first then these young people will be happy and content with what they have and will live in true peace which only Jesus Christ can offer.

When I say that children understand more than their parents think they do, I always give an example from within my own family. I never spoke of the apparitions to my daughter Marija as I thought she was still too little to understand. One day, when she was only two years old, Marija was playing with her friend in her room and I was looking in on them. Her friend told her, among other things, that her mother can drive a car. Marija remained quiet for a while and then said, "So what, my mom speaks with Gospa every single day." Even though I never said anything to her, she noticed something was going on in our home. Do you see how important a parent's example can be?

Gospa also asks that we fast on bread and water every Wednesday and Monday. I am aware that many of you do not like to fast and that it is one of the most difficult requests Gospa asks of us. There are many nice anecdotes, concerning this, which I came across talking to many pilgrims from all over the world. Even though we are very similar we are also very different in our comprehension of certain things. For instance, if I tell an American that we need to fast on bread and water he or she always asks me if they are at least allowed to drink their morning coffee. I answer them by telling them that they can drink coffee in the morning but to do it before Gospa wakes up so that She does not see them. Italians, on the other hand, ask me if they can have lunch instead of dinner. Some even ask me how many hours on a Wednesday must they fast for, as if they do not know how many hours a Wednesday has! Many people try to evade fasting one way or another. Gospa is very clear on the matter. To fast means to fast on bread and water! She does not ask of the truly sick to fast. Those who have headaches or stomach aches are not considered as truly sick. The truly sick are those who suffer heavy and chronic illnesses. Through prayer the ill can learn what else they can do to substitute fasting. The rest of us can pray to God to help us fast the way Gospa wishes us to fast. The ability to fast is a grace given to us by God.

Our Mother also wants us to confess at least once a month. She specifically said that there is not a man or woman on earth that is not in the need of a monthly confession. It is also important that the Bible returns to our homes. We need to read it every day because it is the living word of God.

When Gospa gives me a message, the does not clarify it. She gives it to me as it is conveyed to you. When She asked that the Bible be reintroduced into family life, I interpreted it as a invitation to read at least one or two sentences from the Bible each day. It is not important how much of the Bible is being read, what is important is that the word of God is read within our households. A Bible must not be a souvenir that we never hold in our hands.

After so many years of having apparitions, I gathered some courage and commented on a message which had significant importance to me, in the presence of Gospa: "Dear children, renew the Church!" As did the rest, I too felt frightened of such an important task. I asked Her, "Who are we to renew the Church?

Why, Mother, do you ask this of us? What can we possibly do?" She answered by saying, "Dear children, first renew yourselves, your families and I will help you to renew others. I ask you now – renew yourselves, all of you. Renew your families and then you will be able to renew others."

Today is also a special day for me because I saw Her face and felt Her closeness. Many pilgrims ask me what it is like to be in the presence of Gospa. I can describe this only through one example. I am also a mother and I have two children. As any normal mother, I too would sacrifice my life for my children. However, when I am with Gospa it is as if my children do not exist. All I feel is a yearning for Her to take me with Her so that I may forever look at Her face and feel Her near me. You can imagine how difficult it is once She leaves and we need to go on with our daily lives. For this reason, after every apparition, I retreat to my room to pray for as long as it is necessary for me to understand and accept that this is how it needs to be and that, through prayer, I receive strength to carry on with my everyday life. There is a constant thought I have: my dear God, how nice it is in Heaven and how nice it is to look at Her forever! And Her Son Jesus even more so!

Looking at all of you here with all your flags – from Croatia, Italy, Germany, Spain... – I wish to make you aware of Gospa's calls so that we may all gather underneath Her flag. I would love it if we could all fight for Her, for love and peace, for what She requests of us. Although She has been coming to Medjugorje for years, not once did our Mother say, "Dear, Croats!" She always says, "My dear children!" This means that all of us are Her children. One day when we stand before God, before His holy face, he will not ask what were we like as Croats, what were we like as Italians or as Germans; He will ask us what were we like as humans, what our souls were like.

I am often asked to explain what Medjugorje represents to me. In order for me to answer this question, I need to use a simple example. While I was climbing Cross Mountain one day, there was a group of Italian pilgrims also climbing. They were ahead of me. They were carrying a very ill young man on a stretcher. Those who have climbed Cross Mountain know how steep it is and how difficult it is to carry someone up on a stretcher. They were relentless. It was difficult but they had smiles on their faces. Later on, they were approached by a group of German pilgrims and they offered to carry the young man although they neither knew him nor any of the Italian pilgrims. They carried him up Cross Mountain for a while and then came across some American pilgrims who took over from the German pilgrims. The ill young man was brought to the top of the mountain – carried by the hands of the world. This is what Medjugorje represents to me! I urge you all to unite under Gospa's flag of peace and love and I urge you to fight for our brothers and sisters who have not yet learned of this love. Trust me, this is how we ourselves can achieve happiness too, for this is also a prayer for ourselves.
Thank you!

"Dear children,
whenever you pray for others
you are praying for yourselves,
for your future."

Although she has been coming to Medjugorje for years, not once did our Mother say, "Dear Croats!" She says, "My dear children!" This means that all people are Her children.

"My children, pray with your hearts. Every prayer from the heart is a good prayer. Feel the love for them in your hearts first. Think of them as your brothers and sisters who were not as fortunate as you have been to learn of God's love. When you feel this for them, then you can pray for them. Do not criticize or judge them. Love them, pray for them and be examples of how one should live. This is how you shall change them. This is how you shall help them and how you shall wipe away the tears I shed for them."

"Dear children, if you need to choose between Holy Mass and an apparition, always choose Holy Mass, for my Son is with you then."

"Dear children,
first renew yourselves,
your families and
I will help you
renew others."

ITALIANO

"Dear children, I invited you,
open your hearts,
let me in so that I
may make apostles of you."

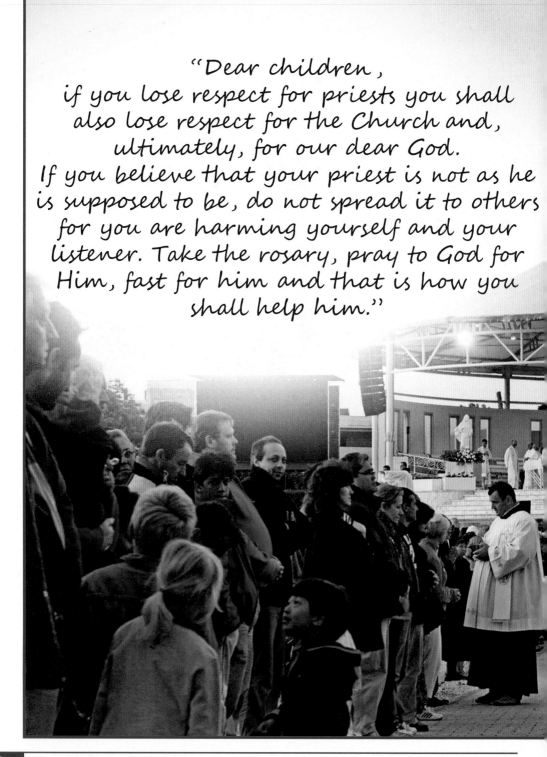

"Dear children,
if you lose respect for priests you shall
also lose respect for the Church and,
ultimately, for our dear God.
If you believe that your priest is not as he
is supposed to be, do not spread it to others
for you are harming yourself and your
listener. Take the rosary, pray to God for
Him, fast for him and that is how you
shall help him."

"Dear children, renew the Church!"

The School of Gospa
Ivan Dragićević's Testimony

Ivan Dragićević was born on the 25th of May 1965, in Bijakovići, Parish of Medjugorje. He has daily apparitions to this day. He has received nine secrets from Gospa. He is married and has four children. He lives with his family in the United States of America as well as in Medjugorje. His prayer intent entrusted to him by Gospa is to pray for the youth and priests.

PRAY, PRAY, PRAY!

Praised be Jesus and Mary! Dear friends, I extend my heartfelt greetings to all of you. I am happy that I can share the joy of togetherness with all of you. Two seers and I still have apparitions and we do not know until when they will last. Gospa says, "I have presented myself here as the Queen of Peace. I call upon you to pray and fast for peace, to renew prayer within your homes and to accept my blessing."

Gospa's messages call for the praying of the Rosary, for the participation in Holy Mass, for confession, for reading the Bible and for adoration of the Blessed Sacrament. The tradition of the Church is recognized in these acts. We are asked many times why Gospa speaks so much of what we all already know. She says nothing new and She keeps repeating Herself. The answer is a simple one; Mary is a mother. Every mother repeats to her child the importance of something. There is no mother lucky enough to only have to tell her child something once and have her child listen to her then. This is the same with Gospa. As our Mother, She too needs to repeat what is important for our salvation.

This relationship can also be compared with the situations at schools or our homes. Children get homework which needs to be completed at home. Many children would forget to do their homework if their mother did not remind them to learn, work, write... Mothers do not give their children new homework to do, she only reminds the child of its obligations. Gospa acts like this with us too. We know what we need to do, how to live but She sees that we do not do what we are supposed to be doing. This is the reason She is with us for so long and reminds us of our tasks. In the monthly messages She always highlights what we should think of during that specific month. This then becomes our prayer intention. As the monthly messages are of great importance, we call them the Lessons of Gospa or the School of Gospa.

During an apparition on one of the anniversaries Mary said, "I invite you to pray. Dear children, whoever prays needs not to be afraid of their future. Forget not that I am with you and that I love you. Pray, pray, pray!" Although peace is the reason for Mary's apparitions, She speaks more of prayer than She does of peace. This is also a lesson. Prayer is the only path to true peace. Everything Gospa says about prayer can be broken down into four points: prayer, fasting, confession and Bible reading.

The first thing Mary asks for is to find time for prayer. Nothing bad can derive from prayer. However, many Catholics declare that they do not have time to pray. Whoever claims this is telling a grave lie. People who pray have the same 24 hour day as those who do not pray. They still have enough time left to do everything that those who do not have time to pray do. So, the problem is not time, the problem is the lack of love. If there is no love, there is no time. If there is love, we will find time for those dear to us. This is why Gospa prays for non-believers on the second of every month so that they may learn of God's love. The problem of lack of time is easily solved when the problem of lack of love is solved.

Many of us have experienced God's love because Gospa prayed that we start praying. Our Mother also asks us to pray for non-believers. Those who state that God does not exist are not the only non-believers. Those who believe in God but do not pray are also considered to be non-believers.

Mary constantly asks us to pray individually, with our families and in groups. Common sense tells us that personal prayer comes first for only an individual willing to pray can take part in family or group prayer. This individual can also encourage family prayer and found prayer groups.

How are prayer groups formed? If an individual sincerely decides to pray, he or she is bound to meet someone who is also willing to pray the Rosary with him or her, to read the Bible and to talk about the secrets of sacred faith. When two people pray together we already have a prayer group formed. This prayer group will soon be joined by others who are also willing to pray and soon the group grows larger. I do not need to stress what a prayer group means for humanity.

A person needs to pray alone if he or she wishes to stay in the spirit of prayer but he or she also needs to find time for family prayer. Gospa especially calls for this. It is also important that parents and their children pray together.

Mary also wishes to change the reasons and motivations for praying. Many people only pray when they need something. They pray for some time and often think: if God makes my prayer come true, that's fine. If He doesn't give me what I asked for, well, I did what I had to but nothing happened so it's not my fault. This motivation for praying is selfish. It is not Christian. In one of Her messages to us Gospa said, "Seek God not by your needs but for His love!" If we seek for God because He loves us then the problem of lack of time for prayer will be solved. When we start praying like this we will be able to pray for everything else.

I will explain with an example: if parents devote themselves to their children only when their children need something then they will not feel good. Children need to feel their parents' love all the time and parents need to feel that same love from their children. We often talk about how parents need to kiss their children more often but it is rarely mentioned that parents need to feel the love of their children too. The latter is also important. This is how Gospa wishes to raise us in connection to our relationship with God. Seek God because He is our Father, because He loves us! If we turn to Him with this state of mind and with sincere love then He will surely give us everything we need. Mary asks that we pray from the heart.

Many wonder what that means; to pray from the heart. It means to pray from love and with love. This kind of prayer has two levels. The first level can be reached instantly. For example, Gospa calls for me to pray from the heart today and I say, "I don't know how to pray from the heart!" Yet, I do what She asks of me. I take the Bible, a cross, a prayer book, a rosary and I start to pray. I do so every single day, despite whether or not I receive anything and despite the state of my mind. I stay faithful to Gospa's call believing that my prayer is from the heart because I know I did everything within my means. If I do this then I can reach the second level of prayer. The second level is growth in prayer, hope, love, peace and prayer spirit.

If a florist is asked when a flower will open and blossom the florist will probably answer by saying that she does not know but that she has done everything she could so it would one day. The florist prepared the soil, watered the plant and overlooked its growth but she does not have the power to make the flower open. This can be compared to the parable of Jesus about the Sower and the Seed. The sower planted the same seed but each seed did not grow equally. The same happens if we pray with the heart. If we do everything we can then we shall be rewarded with abundant fruits.

Gospa says that those who pray should not fear the future. If we pray with the heart and meet with God, our Father, then we shall not be afraid of the future for sure. On the contrary, we shall look at our past, present and future fearlessly. We know that whoever feels fear wishes to get rid of that feeling. Some try to get rid of it by drinking alcohol or by abusing drugs while others get rid through prayer. We sometimes act like lazy children whose mothers need to constantly remind them to study. Often, these children start to study because their mothers told them to do so and because they feel that they do it for their mothers. We often act like this toward Gospa. She does not call for us to pray because of Her, She does it for our sakes. Our Mother knows what we need. Therefore, we need to answer Her calls. I have met many people who have truly listened to Gospa's calls. She tells us that we will not regret doing what She advises in Her messages. She once said, "Dear children, life on earth is not eternal, it is like a pilgrimage." Each of us needs to ask ourselves what is standing in our way to eternity. Mary asks us to discover God in our daily prayers and that He becomes our joy. The sincerer we pray, the sooner He will become our joy. Gospa repeats, "Pray, pray, pray!" We will be able to recognise our needs through prayer.

Knowledge of God is not the problem, the problem is love. Only love can motivate man to do God's will. Many people today have become indifferent and do not care whether God exists or not – they live their lives without giving God a second thought. There is also one other type of non-believers. These are the ones that know that God exists, know what God has said, know His Commandments but do not practice their religion.

We too can be put in this group of non-believers because we know what we have to do but we do not do it. We know for sure that not a single atheist will pray the Rosary today but we can be even more sure that many Catholics will not pray the Rosary today either. Not a single atheist went to church on Sunday but neither did many Catholics. When it comes to practising our faith, there is little difference.

This is the reason Gospa calls for us to experience God's love in order to do what we know and need to do. Those who have started to pray, confess and have converted in Medjugorje need to know that this is the grace that Gospa has been praying for on their behalves. These people have also become the driving force of Medjugorje, as they have passed from knowledge of God to practicing their faith. Not a single Christian who has been to Medjugorje has ever said that he or she does not know how to pray but many of them have said that they have started praying once they came to Medjugorje. The answer to the question of why Gospa started to appear lies here.

Many say that Gospa keeps repeating Herself in Her messages, that She keeps telling us what we already know. They say, "We have the Bible, we have the Sacraments, we have the Church…Why do we need the apparitions? Why has Gospa been appearing for so long?" It is true, we do have the Church, the Bible, and the Sacraments but it is also true that we do not live in accordance with what the Bible says, what the Church teaches as well as with what the Sacraments say. This is why Gospa comes. She come to help us truly live in accordance with Christian values.

Many do not like it when She constantly keeps asking us to pray. A friend of mine said, "It cannot be Gospa. She's always repeating Herself and tells us to 'pray, pray, pray'. In the Bible, Mary is quiet most of the time but now She keeps repeating Herself." I ran into him recently and he said, "I know what the latest message says: pray, pray, pray." I said, "My dear friend, I also know of this message," but then I asked him if he had started to pray. He was not sure of what to say so I said, "Thank you, dear friend, for your answer. Now I know why Gospa keeps repeating Herself. If you had started praying today, I'm sure Gospa would not have repeated Herself again. Maybe She would have said something new today." The same applies to you. If Gospa again repeats Herself and says, "Pray, pray, pray", you too shall be responsible for this.

When Gospa asks us to pray for the ill we can say, "Thank God I am healthy but I will pray for the ill." When She asks us to pray for the youth, we can say, "I am not young anymore but I shall pray for the young." However, when She asks us to pray to experience God's love, none of us can say, "I have enough of His love, I don't need anymore." It is necessary not only to experience His love through life but through eternity too. We can never say that we have enough of it. One day, when we come to Heaven, we will understand and see how far from eternity we were and what God's love meant for our salvation.

Gospa does not only ask that we pray; She wants our lives to become a prayer. I remember a pilgrim once heard that Gospa asked that prayer groups pray for three hours. She found this odd and thought that it was impossible that Gospa was asking for this. A year later, the same pilgrim returned to Medjugorje and asked me again whether Gospa was still asking that prayer groups pray for three hours so I said, "I'm sorry dear lady, you are too late. Gospa no longer asks for three-hour long prayers, now She asks for twenty-four-hour-long prayers." She said, "Well, ok, then I'll still keep on praying for three hours." Do you see what a wise mother and teacher Gospa is? Can our lives be a prayer? They can, because Gospa, like God, does not ask for the impossible. No where in the Bible will you read, "Fly like birds!" Why? Because it is impossible. However, Gospa keeps telling us to forgive, to love, to be merciful and to pray. Jesus also said, "Pray constantly!" This is possible.

We need to clearly understand what prayer is. Prayer is a meeting with God. Whenever a family prays, it meets with God. Whenever you pray the Rosary, you meet with Jesus. Whenever you confess, you meet with a forgiving God. Whenever you attend Holy Mass, you meet with God who gives us His body as food. Whenever you read the Bible, you meet with God who talks to you and whenever you realize His gifts to you, you again meet with Him. For example, motherhood is a gift. Devotion in raising your children also means to meet with God. Actually, whatever we do can mean a meeting with God. Unfortunately, today there is so much restlessness, selfishness, greed – many things that can interfere in our relationship with God. Gospa does not want us to pray and then spend the rest of our day in impiety. She asks for our love for God. Everything else shall come on its own.

Everyone sees that many Christians have a wrong perception of their relationship with God. Now is the time when man must meet with God and establish a proper relationship with Him, for it determines each individual's fate. The situation today is alarming. Mankind wants to be independent of everything, even of God. Therefore it is a logical question when one asks whether there is hope for a better future in the world we live in. There is hope, but only under one condition: that we reconnect with God again. If this does not happen, man will drift further away from God and enter into a dark world of hatred, loneliness and inability which will then lead to overall destruction.

Dear friends, may the days you spend in Medjugorje be a time of your spiritual renewal. When you go home, do not stop, continue with the spiritual renewal of your families. Together with Gospa I will pray for all of you, for your intents, your needs and your families. Dear friends, together with our Mother, the Queen of Peace, let us pray for peace in the world!

Let us become tools in God's hands. Let us be apostles who will carry Her messages to the world! Only those who live by God's will can become apostles.

In the Gospel Jesus often says, "Do not fear!" Gospa also often repeats and says, "Do not fear, dear children, I am with you!" Let us opt for peace, for God, for in Him is our only and true peace.

Dear friends, may God bless you all! Peace be with you and your families! Thank you!

"I invite you to pray. Dear children, who prays needs not to fear the future. Do not forget, I am with you and I love you. Pray, pray, pray!"

"Fear not, dear children, I am with you!"

"Seek God
not because of your needs
but because of His love!"

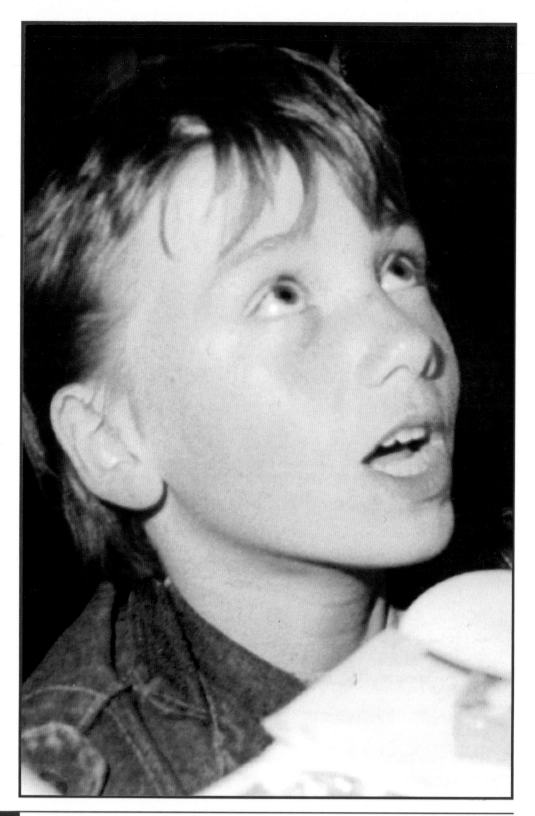

The Answers to all Important Questions Through Prayer
Jakov Čole's Testimony

Jakov Čolo was born on the 6th of March 1971, in Sarajevo. He had daily apparitions from the 26th of June 1981, till the 12th of September 1998. On that day, after receiving the 10th secret, Gospa told him that he would have apparitions once a year throughout his entire life, on Christmas. Jakov is married, has three children and lives with his family in Medjugorje. Jakov Čolo prays for the sick.

FAST, ESPECIALLY ON WEDNESDAYS AND FRIDAYS!

I greet you all and I thank our dearest God and Heavenly Mother for the days you spend in Medjugorje; singing and praying. I know you could have been somewhere else, resting in nice resorts, but you chose to come to Medjugorje. You have chosen well! This is the right place to be in, a place where you can meet with God, where Gospa appears; a place where you can feel our Mother's unconditional love! I thank you for this from the bottom of my heart!

It is my intent to give a testimony of my apparitions. When Gospa started appearing to me in Medjugorje, I was ten years old. Before this, I used to live like any other child in Medjugorje. I did not think of God that much. I attended Holy Mass, prayed but I did not take it as seriously as I do now. When I saw Gospa for the first time, especially when I saw Her loving eyes, and when I felt how much She loves me and that She is my Mother, I experienced something special, something that cannot be described in words. Deep within myself, I felt my life was just beginning to start.

What else could I say to Gospa but "yes" after that? All I can do is let Her lead me. Gospa wishes to lead me, as She does all Her other children, to the final goal, to Jesus Christ. Medjugorje is actually Gospa's school. From the very beginning, She has been trying to teach us how to truly live and whom to turn to. From the beginning, She has given us messages, called upon us to pray, to convert, to make peace, to fast and to celebrate Holy Mass. As a ten year old boy, I asked myself whether I would be able to answer Her calls and live the way She wanted me to live. It is crystal clear to me now: if you truly love somebody the way I love Gospa and our saviour Jesus Christ, then nothing is difficult. Gospa confirms this in Her messages to us. She says, "Dear children, it is enough just to open your hearts, I will do the rest."

Honestly, Medjugorje is the place where we should all say "yes" to Gospa and to live by Her advice, starting today. We should all say, "Starting today, Gospa, I wish to celebrate your Son as the centre of my life."

Gospa invites us to pray every single day. It is important to pray the Rosary every day. Our Mother always keeps saying that prayer can give us the answer to all important questions in life. Many pilgrims ask me questions I will never be able to answer. However, Gospa teaches us that we can realize what is important through prayer. She also calls upon us to pray with our families and to let God be the centre of our families. If God is present in our family then it will truly become a sacred family. Many of Gospa's messages talk about this. She says, "I wish for you to be holy, for your families to become sacred."

What could be nicer than for you to return to your families back home and say, "I want to pray with you. From today, I wish to have God with us. From today, I want our family to have time for God." This would be the nicest gift we could give our Mother!

She also invites us to fast, especially on Wednesdays and Fridays. What should fasting look like? Our Mother wants us to pray out of love, in silence. I believe that not everybody needs to know when we are fasting; we should do it quietly. Many say that it is hard to fast but I have already said that nothing is difficult if you love someone. Why do we need to pray? Remember, Gospa said that we can accomplish anything when we pray and fast. We can stop wars. There's your reason for fasting!

Where do people err the most? People come across difficult times during their lives and that is when people often say, "God, where are You? Why do You not help me?" Instead, we should ask ourselves, "How have I behaved up to now? How much of my time did I devote to God? How much did I pray? How did I raise my children? What kind of an example did I set for them? What did I do to alleviate the evil in the world?" God is always with us but, unfortunately, we often do not want Him there. We should put our lives and everything that is happening to us into God's hands.

I know many young people who have entered into marriage. Some of them say that they do not wish to have children straight away, that they want to enjoy themselves and be on their own for a while. Then they need to pay the loans on their houses and then spend time with each other again. In the end, they say that they only want one child. This is a typical example of how people do not surrender their lives to God. We wish to make decisions on our own and when we find ourselves in difficult situations we do not know how to react. Those who have surrendered their lives into God's hands always know the right answer and know how to react in certain situations.

Gospa constantly asks us to convert. I tell all the pilgrims who come to Medjugorje that they should not come because of the visionaries or because they wish to receive a sign. The greatest gift we can receive in Medjugorje is to convert, to start a new life with God. God gives new life to our families too. Therefore, Medjugorje does not end here; it continues to live in your homes. It is not enough to say that you have been to Medjugorje. It is necessary that others see and recognise the spirit of Medjugorje within you, that they feel God's work through you. This is the true image and purpose of Medjugorje. Simply said, yet difficult to do, we need to talk less and act more. When we talk about ourselves we are all good people but, in reality, it is often not so. We always need to ask ourselves whether we are acting in accordance with what we say.

Gospa came to Medjugorje as the Queen of Peace but She also says, "Dear children, if you do not have peace in your hearts, then you cannot pray for peace." She always tells us to first pray for peace in our hearts for there is nothing more valuable than the feeling of peace and love within our own hearts. There is nothing nicer than when a person loves another person, when we can extend a hand to one another.

Our faith teaches us this and Gospa only wishes to help us understand this. It is easy to love friends and family but we need to love all people. We need to see Jesus in every human being. We especially need to pray for those who do not believe in God and who have not yet felt His love. We need to be examples for them.

Before leaving for home, you should promise God and Gospa today that you will change your lives, that you will start living with God, that you will be examples to others and that you will talk of God's love and goodness to all people. Our Heavenly Mother encourages us to do this.

Although She has been appearing for so many years in Medjugorje, we are still not aware of the grace She has given us. For whom does She come? She comes for us, because She is our Mother, because She loves us immensely. In one of Her messages She said, "Dear children, if only you knew how much I love you you would cry with joy." That's how much She loves us! Not much is needed for us to love Her too. Let us promise Her today that we shall love Her as our Mother and that we shall love Her for the rest of our lives.

Let us remember one more detail; at the end of every message Gospa says, 'Thank you for having responded to my call." This shows how great She is. We are the ones who should be thanking Her everyday and especially be thanking God for every gift we receive. She says thank you to us! Therefore, let's start praying today to feel God's presence in our hearts and to accept Gospa as our Mother.

I promise to pray for all of you as well as for the ill. I ask you all to do the same for us. Thank you!

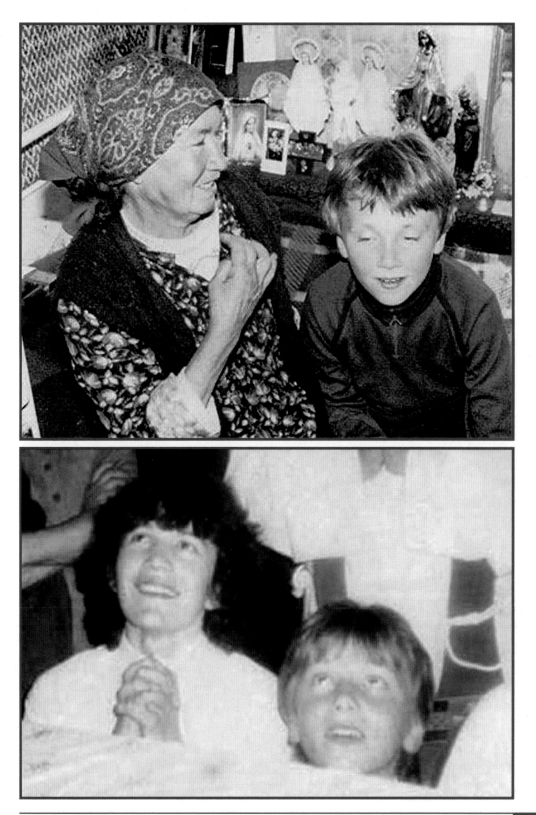

"Dear children,
if you do not have peace in your hearts
then you cannot pray for peace."

"Dear children,
if only you knew how much I love you,
you would cry with joy."

"Thank you
for having responded
to my call."

We are important to God
Marija Pavlović-Lunetti's Testimony

Marija Pavlović-Lunetti was born on the 1st of April 1965, in Bijakovići, Parish of Medjugorje. She still has daily apparitions. Gospa sends messages to the parish and the world through her. She received messages on every Thursday, from the 1st of March 1984, until the 8th of January 1987. Since January 1987, She receives these messages on the 25th of every month. She has received ten secrets from Gospa. Marija is married and has four children. She lives with her family both in Italy and Medjugorje. She prays for the souls in purgatory.

DO NOT TALK ABOUT FASTING, START FASTING!

From the very beginning, our Mother encourages us to truly live each day as it if were our last. While we were still children, us seers realized that holiness is achieved now, not in the future. Therefore I urge you to use this time of grace for prayer as this our Mother's wish. We will understand God better through prayer, we will better understand the reality we are living in and we will understand our mission in this world. I am sure there are many among you who think about what to do and what your future will be like. You can find the answers in Gospa's words and message She has repeated several times, "Those who pray need not fear the future." This is how we started to pray and now we are no longer afraid of the future, for God is with us.

We live in a consumerist society. An individual is considered as worthy and important as the amount of money he or she makes and spends. Gospa, however, tells us that we are all important in God's salvation project. She encourages us to place God first within our families. When we do this we will surely feel the will for Heaven.

Gospa constantly encouraged us to read the Bible everyday. We did so and then She gradually made us stronger and more open to testify of our experiences. Although we took Her advice and prayed in the privacy of our rooms in silence, we felt the need to testify of God's love. Our testimony became more convincing thanks to prayer. We felt a deep joy and will to live differently. I wish that all of you live in accordance with what Gospa asks of us and already lead heavenly lives here on earth.

Seeing that us visionaries felt this need from the very beginning, we often felt nostalgic and the need to see Gospa. Every time Gospa would appear we wanted the apparition to be a long one because it is really nice to be with Gospa. We said to each other, "Why don't we live the way Gospa wishes us to live now, on earth? Live better, more profoundly and with a purpose." It is necessary to choose holiness. True Christians should live holy during every situation: within their family, within their parishes, at school, at work and wherever God sends them.

In one of Her messages Gospa said, "Do not talk about fasting, start fasting!" That is how we started to fast. Our Mother first asked us to fast on Fridays and then gradually She started encouraging us to stop watching TV, drinking alcohol, smoking cigarettes... This is how the young men from our prayer group stopped drinking alcohol and stopped smoking and started to pray and fast more concretely.

Gospa also asked us to pray. We first prayed the Credence, seven Our Fathers, Hail Mary's and Glory Be's. Then She asked us to pray the Rosary, all three parts (now, thanks to Pope John Paul II, we have four parts). Gradually, She asked for prayer groups to pray for three hours. Little by little, She asked that our lives become prayers. This is how our true conversion began. We need to keep changing our lives every single day.

This means that everyday we should say, "Dear Lord, I offer this day, all the people I meet and everything I experience to You; bless it all."

When Gospa told us that Heaven, hell and Purgatory exist we said to everybody, "Do you know that spirituality is also important, not only material things? We do not depend only on food to live, we also depend on God's word. Our souls need prayer and conversion." Therefore, I urge all of you to think about your spiritual lives.

I remember when Gospa talked about confession for the first time. It was during Her second apparition to us. It was 10:30 PM when She appeared and She allowed all those who were present to touch Her. We asked Her how could we touch Her? How was it possible? She replied, "Take the hands of those people who do not see me and guide them towards me." We did as She asked and we told the people that they were allowed to touch Her. All of the people touched Her and felt something. Some of them felt cold, some of them felt warmth, some of them felt as if an electric current went through their bodies and some of them felt a smell similar to the smell of roses. All of them believed Gospa was present. While the people were touching Gospa we, the visionaries, saw stains appearing on Her dress. Some of the stains were larger than others. We started to cry. We asked Her why Her dress was so dirty and She told us that the stains that appeared on Her dress were the sins of the people who touched Her. She told us to confess our sins. From that moment onwards, we started going to confession and truly started converting. Each of us chose a priest to be our spiritual leader and we started growing in faith.

The feeling that we were important to God also started to grow. Imagine, God had chosen us so that thousands and thousands of people would be saved through us! We had a need to tell everybody we met how important we were because Gospa had told us so. We are part of God's plan. He wants to bring many people closer to Him through us. This is why Gospa keeps encouraging us to convert and choose holiness. When man decides to become holy, he or she becomes an extended hand of God for his or her family, their parish and the place they live in.

During the first years of the apparitions, Fr. Jozo Zovko repeatedly told us that Gospa invites all of us. I will also repeat what he said: we are all invited, we are all chosen. To those who doubt by asking whether or not God really exists, I can only say that during the first days of the apparitions I felt the love of God so intensely, not only through Gospa but through prayer and everyday life. I simply felt that God was with me. I have this feeling to this day. He is not somewhere up in the sky not caring for what becomes of us. On the contrary, He is our everlasting travel companion and feels for us.

As soon as the news of the apparitions came out many pilgrims and sick people started coming to Medjugorje. We interceded and prayed for them before Gospa. We witnessed how people in wheelchairs got up and started to walk. We would talk among each other and wonder whose prayers were responsible for these miracles – were they the result of our prayers for them, the prayers of other people, or even the result of Gospa's prayers for them. Slowly, we started growing in our faith and started recognizing and thanking God for everything He did with us, through us and through all those who came to Medjugorje and gave testimonies of Gospa's love. We felt God's presence in a special way; we felt Him close by, with us and knew that He is always present in our lives. We are thankful to Gospa for helping us feel God's love.

Whenever I pray for those who seek my prayers I say, "Please, dear Mother, help them understand and accept the fact that life is short and not let them waste their lives on irrelevant matters, help them grow in holiness." When we decide to do so, fear of the future disappears, all we feel is profound joy because of God's presence and love. I wish to invite you to this joy, to use the time which has been given to you so mercifully. Gospa is with us and constantly keeps telling us, "I intercede before God for you." She repeats what She used to say in Cana of Galilee, "Do what He asks of you!"

Do not be afraid of God, Gospa, praying or anything that comes as a result of this because, as Gospa says, you will feel the joy and the need to spread this joy onto others. May our Almighty Father bless all of you and may the Queen of Peace protect and intercede for you. I will pray for you all!

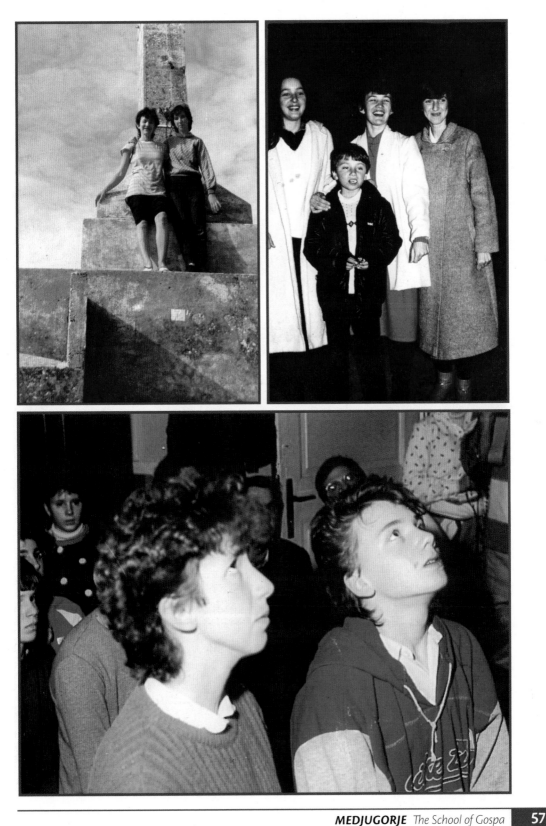

Do not be afraid of God,
Gospa, praying or anything
that comes as a result of
this because, as Gospa says,
you will feel the joy and the
need to spread this joy
onto others.

"Please,
dear Mother, help them
understand and accept the fact that
life is short and not let them waste their
lives on irrelevant matters, help them
grow in holiness." When we decide
to do so, fear of the future disappears,
all we feel is profound joy because
of God's presence and love.

Strong faith and persistent prayer
Vicka Ivanković-Mijatović's Testimony

Vicka Ivanković-Mijatović was born on the 3rd of September 1964, in Bijakovići, Parish of Medjugorje. She has daily apparitions to this day. She received nine secrets from Gospa. Vicka is married, has two children and lives in Krehin Gradac, close to Medjugorje. She prays for the sick.

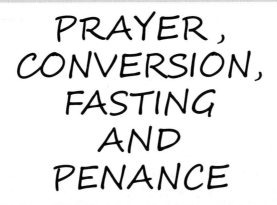

PRAYER, CONVERSION, FASTING AND PENANCE

Dear pilgrims, dear friends, first of all I would like to greet all of you with all my heart. I am overjoyed to have the opportunity to convey the contents of the most important messages Gospa sends through me to all people. The core of these messages is prayer, conversion, fasting, penance and peace. Gospa invites us to reflect over and pray all three parts of Gospa's Rosary – the Joyful, Sorrowful and Glorious Mysteries everyday. She also encourages us to fast on bread and water on Wednesdays and Fridays. Strong faith is what She yearns for the most.

When She speaks of prayer, Gospa does not mean that She wishes us to just pronounce some words; She wants us to open our hearts, day in and day out, so that God's grace could enter them. Therefore, before you start praying, clear your mind of all thoughts distracting you and then start praying Our Father. While pronouncing the words of the prayer, focus your thoughts on our great Father in heaven, who is full of immeasurable love and who loves all of us. Tell Him all about your wishes and problems. Ask for His will to be done. May His will be done and not yours. Afterwards, pray Hail Mary and also concentrate on what you are saying. With your hearts, look at Mary as a great Mother who is with us always and who loves us tremendously. Then pray Glory Be. Be sincere in celebrating your Father, His Son and the Holy Spirit. Thank the Holy Trinity for everything they have given you, for the good and the bad. Pray to God so that you may accept everything that comes from Him. Open your hearts every single day over and over again and meditate over every word you say.

Gospa gives us a magnificent example of this; everybody who has a vase with flowers pours a few drops of water in it everyday. The flowers grow and develop until they become beautiful. This also happens to our hearts. If we water our hearts with a few drops of prayer everyday, they too will grow and develop. If we do not water our hearts, we will feel them withering away. Unfortunately this happens too often. When the time for prayer comes, we often say, "Oh, I can't do it today, I'll leave it for tomorrow." This then happens again tomorrow, after tomorrow and the next day and then our hearts become filled with bad contents instead of filling with prayer. Praying with the heart cannot be learnt or studied. It is realized step by step, living by God's will each day.

Whenever Gospa recommends fasting on bread and water, She always emphasizes that She does not wish the ill to fast. She advises the ill to give up something they like most. The rest of us should fast out of love for Jesus and His Mother. In order to do this, we need strong will power.

Gospa invites us to complete conversion by saying, "Dear children, whenever you have problems or are having hard times you think that Jesus and I are far from you. We are always close. All you need to do is open your hearts and realize how much we love you." Our Mother would be overjoyed if we truly refrain from sin.

In connection to this She says, "I give you my peace and love so that you may share it with your family and friends." She blesses us and prays for this.

We would make our Mother very happy if we start praying the Rosary with our families again. If parents pray with their children Satan cannot harm them in any way. Gospa constantly repeats that Satan is very strong and wishes to distract us and keep us from doing any good. This is why She wants us to pray even more. The best way to repel Satan's attacks is to pray the Rosary. The Rosary is the most effective weapon to use against the father of all lies. Therefore, Gospa advises us that it is best to carry something blessed on your person: a cross, a medallion, or any other religious object.

However, the centre of our lives should be Holy Mass. It is the most important and most sacred moment, a moment when the living Jesus comes and whom we receive in Holy Communion. Gospa wants us to especially prepare ourselves for this moment so that we can receive Jesus deservingly. In order for this to be realized, we need to go to monthly confessions or to confess according to our needs. Confession should not be taken lightly. It is wrong to confess and then keep living the way we did before confession. We need to change ourselves; we need to become new persons.

Gospa especially worries about the youth of today as they are in a very difficult situation. We can help them by loving them and praying for them. Our Mother says, "Dear youth, what the world offers today is not eternal. Satan takes advantage of every situation in order to realize his poisonous plan for he wants to destroy your families and you." However, this is also a time of grace. We should become aware of Gospa's messages and start living them.

Many of you know that Gospa took Jakov and me to see Heaven, hell and Purgatory. It happened when the apparitions had just begun. Jakov and I were alone at his house. Gospa came and told us that we were going to see Heaven, hell and Purgatory. Jakov became scared and said, "Dear Gospa, take Vicka, she has the most brothers and sisters. I am an only child." He thought that Gospa was going to take us with Her for good and that we would not be returning. I, on the other hand, was thinking about how many days it would take us to get there and which roads we were going to use.

Then, Gospa took us by our hands, me by the right and Jakov by the left, and we went with Her. The ceiling above our heads simply parted, just enough for us to pass through. Before we knew it, we were in Heaven. There was no end to Heaven and it was lighten up with a light that cannot be seen on earth. The people we saw there were happy. They were all dressed in either grey, pink or yellow dresses. They were walking, praying, singing and there were little angles flying over them. Gospa then said, "Do you see how happy people in Heaven are?" Truly, the happiness those people feel in Heaven cannot be felt on earth.

Purgatory is also a large place but people there cannot be seen clearly. Everything was grey, ash-colored. We could feel the people there twitching, bobbing and thumping. Gospa said that we need to pray for them a lot in order for them to leave Purgatory. There is a great fire in the centre of hell.

We first saw people there in their normal forms but after they would enter the fire they would reemerge in the form of animals. It seemed like they were never human. The deeper they went into the fire the more fervently they would talk against God. Gospa told us that people who were in hell went there at their own free will, because they wanted to. People on earth who act opposite to God's will are already living in hell; later, they just continue what they started on earth. Many think that there is nothing after life on earth and therefore let go and live sinful lives. However, they are very wrong to think so for we are only passers-by on earth and life continues in eternity.

I shall intercede for you and your families before our heavenly Mother. May you all be blessed through Her by our kind and almighty God. Think of us, the seers, in your prayers sometimes.

One morning, two months before the apparitions began, Vicka's brother, Franjo, was preparing his tools to go wood chopping when he came across two wooden rosaries on his cultivator. Surprised, he brought them to his mother and she told him to ask around and to try find out who lost them so that they could be returned to their owner. In the meantime, the apparitions began and no one had come forward looking for the rosaries. Vicka's mother and grandmother told Vicka to ask Gospa about the rosaries. This is what Gospa said, "It is a gift from me to your family!"

All those who have started to pray,
confess, convert in Medjugorje must know that
it is a grace given to them
through Gospa's prayers.

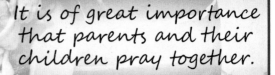

It is of great importance
that parents and their
children pray together.

If there is no love,
there is no time.
If there is love,
time for those whom
we love shall be found.

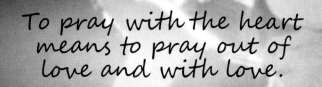

To pray with the heart
means to pray out of
love and with love.

"Dear children,
life on earth is not eternal,
it is like a pilgrimage."

Gospa repeated for three times,
"Pray, pray, pray!"
Through prayer we will know what
we need and what we do not need.

Gospa of Medjugorje – The Queen of Peace, by Croatian artist Krešimir Ledić

GOSPA'S APPARITIONS THROUGHOUT HISTORY
Heaven Could Not Stay Silent
Fr. Karlo Lovrić

Fr. Karlo Lovrić was born on the 2nd of December 1941, in Uzarići where he also attended primary school. He completed junior grammar high school in Široki Brijeg and in 1957 enrolled into a Franciscan grammar high school in Sinj. He continued his education in Dubrovnik with the Jesuits where he graduated. After completing obligatory army service, in 1963 he changed into his Franciscan cloak and started his novitiate in Humac. Fr. Karlo studied philosophy and theology in Visoko, continued his studies in Sarajevo and completed his studies in Königstein, near Frankfurt a.M., where he was ordained and became a priest on the 29th of June 1968. From 1969 to 1971 he served as a spiritual assistant in Humac and from August 1971, till the end of that year he was in the Croatian Catholic Mission in Zurich. In 1972, he founded and led the Croatian Catholic Mission in St. Gallen in Switzerland and remained there till 1980. From 1980 till 1982, he was parish priest in Široki Brijeg. From September 1982, till December 1988, he stayed in Switzerland. Fr. Karlo arrived in Medjugorje in the middle of May of 2005 and serves as a spiritual guide.

FORGIVENESS DOES NOT MEAN WEAKNESS.

There have been over two thousand apparitions, some of which are Marian apparitions, since the beginning of the Church. These apparitions occurred or are still occurring on all continents. Most of the apparitions took place during the last century, especially during the second half of last century. The most numerous apparitions occurred in France, at least those which were approved and recognized. There were also many apparitions in Italy (the most famous apparition in Italy took place in Syracuse in 1953) but there are many apparitions that have not been approved. All these apparitions: approved, pending approval or apparitions that are not in accordance with the teachings of the Church, either by their fruits or messages, have occurred or are still occurring during times when the Church, as God's people, has suffered or when man, as God's child, has suffered or is still suffering. Did Gospa not appear in Fatima during WWI, when people were starving, not only for daily bread but for Eternal Bread too? It was a time of great hatred between people, during the time of the declaration of the October Revolution in Russia – the age of Communism and rejection of God... So many people felt this on their own skin! It was an age of rejection of God; it was an age of bloodshed! It appeared in Russia in 1917 and spread in our land in 1945!

Queen of peace

Both the Queen of Peace and Heaven could not stay silent. Our Mother needed to speak and console Her children. In other places where Gospa appeared or is still appearing, She introduced Herself as a Woman, a Mother or a Queen. The way She would introduced Herself was "determined" by social and political occurrences as well as by occurrences within the Church. In Pontmain (France) She introduced Herself as the *Mother of Hope*, in Fatima (Portugal) She introduced Herself as the *Queen of the Rosary* and in Lourdes (France) She introduced Herself as the *Immaculate Conception*. By introducing Herself as the Immaculate Conception She defended the recently proclaimed dogma, declared by Pope Pius IX in December of 1854, of the Immaculate Conception of the Blessed Virgin Mary.

She introduced Herself as the *Queen of Peace* in Medjugorje. She warned us of the threat of war in these regions. At the beginning of the apparitions She said, "Peace, peace and only peace." The people understood this message as soon as they felt the smell of gun powder near their houses but it was too late. However, it is praiseworthy to mention that believers gathered more often to pray the Rosary in their villages, streets, churches... Even soldiers carried the rosary. Even though they had heavy armour, they trusted that the Rosary would be more helpful.

In Cuapa (Nicaragua) Gospa introduced Herself there as the Mother of Jesus. In Gietrzwal (Poland) She said, "*I am the Virgin Mary.*" In Nigeria She said, "*I am the Intercessor of all Graces,*" and in Amsterdam She said, "*I am the Mother of all Nations.*" In Beauraing (Belgium) She said, "*I am the Immaculate Virgin.*"

Time will tell

The Medjugorje Phenomenon (Apparitions of Gospa in Medjugorje since 1981!) inspired many, theologians and laymen alike, to write on this topic – about the events in Medjugorje, where Gospa appeared. It is interesting to note that the reactions to this event during the first days in 1981 were positive. Why the positive reactions changed, even of those who, considering their vocation, should not doubt the possibility of an apparition (not to say: the possibility of a supernatural event!) can only be speculated. However, this is not the topic now. Time will tell if the Medjugorje visionaries were telling the truth, if they are telling the truth (as the apparitions are still ongoing) or if someone had manipulated them in order to destroy the country (as the media of the time had said and written) or, God forbid, if they were manipulated into bringing grave damage upon the Church. I know that the devil will not cease at anything, in this case, from using innocent and inexperienced children to seduce many, not only believers but priests too. As every kind and reasonable mother, the Church was cautious when, on the 10th of April, 1991, in Zadar, it issued a declaration on Gospa's apparitions in Medjugorje.

"From the very beginning, the Bishops have been following the events of Medjugorje through the local Bishop, the Bishop's Commission and the Commission of the Bishops' Conference of Yugoslavia for Medjugorje. On the basis of studies made so far, it cannot be affirmed that these matters concern supernatural apparitions or revelations."

"Yet the gathering of the faithful from various parts of the world to Medjugorje, inspired by faith or other motives, require the pastoral attention and care, first of all, of the local Bishop and then of the other Bishops with him, so that in Medjugorje and all connected with it, a healthy devotion towards the Blessed Virgin Mary according to the Church may be promoted..."

This second part of the Zadar Declaration proved to be of great use for pastoral workers in Medjugorje. Although supernatural apparitions cannot be proven (yet!), people who came or were yet to come needed spiritual care. During these thirty years the parish has done everything humanly possible. Could it have done more? Only God and those who have done pastoral work in the parish all these years can say.

Help coming from man is always meagre if the help does not come from above. Even St. Paul did not praise his educational teachings, he praised his weaknesses. What single man could attract so many people from all parts of the world through sermons and spiritual seminars?! People come here from China, Japan, South Korea and other parts of the world to strengthen their faith and to stay here for a few days. What else but the call from Heaven could have attracted them to this secluded Herzegovinian village?

Could it have been the natural beauties of this region? How is it that a "random" visit by a Korean young man to Medjugorje changed his life?! Before coming to Medjugorje he wanted to be a musician yet, upon leaving Medjugorje, he became a Franciscan.

It was wise of the Church not to bring a hurried decision concerning the apparitions of Gospa in Medjugorje. Especially since the apparitions are still ongoing, as the visionaries state. Why hurry? If the apparitions are true, they shall always be true. The truth cannot be silenced or bypassed. The best example of this is a little place in France called Laus. Two hundred and ninety years had gone by before it was approved.

On Sunday, on the 4th of May 2008, Bishop of Gap and Embrun, Monsignor Jean Michel di Falco Leandri, officially approved the supernatural character of the apparitions a poor 17- year- old shepherdess called Benoite Rencurel had in the Shrine of Laus, in the Alps. The apparitions started in 1664 and ended in 1718; lasting for 54 years!

During these years, the shepherdess faithfully attended to her duties: she accepted pilgrims, prayed and worked on the conversion of pilgrims through prayer (confession).

Approved Marian Apparitions

This latest shrine joined other approved and well-known shrines of Gospa in France, such as Paris (1830), La Salette (1846), Lourdes (1858), Pontmain (1871) and Pellvoisin (1876), as well as other approved shrines such as Guadalupe (1531) in Mexico, Knock (1879) in Ireland, Fatima (1917) in Portugal, Beauraing (1932), Banneux (1933) in Belgium, Amsterdam (1945) in the Netherlands, Akita (1973) in Japan, Kibeho (1981) in Ruanda– Africa...

In all above stated places, Church approval came relatively soon. However, every act of approval has to pass "through the mill" as every wrong evaluation could cause irreparable damage to the Church. However, approval of the apparitions of Gospa in Laus was unusual and took very long! A whole 290 years!

What will happen with Gospa's apparitions in Medjugorje? They are still called "alleged apparitions". Will Medjugorje have the same or similar fate as the apparitions in Laus had?

We can only pray and ask the Holy Spirit to guide those who decide upon such matters. Shall approval come in a year, two years, thirty or more years is of no relevance. What matters is that the truth surfaces.

If we believe that the Holy Spirit guides the Church (as believers we must believe this!), then we cannot talk about it as coming late. He is the one who always guides the Church, even when we think that whatever the Church does comes too late.

Is it not the work of the Holy Spirit that makes believers recognize God's doing from the very beginning? Would the small village of Laus in France been approved as a place of Gospa's apparitions if the believers had not felt the presence of God and came there as grateful pilgrims? Even so, not even their coming there would have helped had the poor shepherdess, Benoite, made the story of seeing Gospa up

Gospa Speaks In a Simple Manner

Believers as a whole are not deceived easily. Vox populi – vox Dei (the voice of people, the voice of God)! Although they might be uneducated, when theology is concerned, the simplicit of their faith helps them recognize what could be divine. This is the reason why Gospa often appears to little, uneducated and poor children for they will convey what they saw and heard. Gospa speaks in a simple manner, in a language understood by everyone and this is what baffles the "highly-educated". The "highly-educated" are also baffled by the longevity of the apparitions. Not only do they see the duration of the apparitions as a problem but they see the apparitions themselves as problems. Sometimes even religious truth is considered a problem. As a French thinker once said, "Overcome your passions and it will not be difficult for you to believe."

It seems that regular but true believers are not confused by the duration of Gospa's apparitions. They see Gospa as their Mother. Rightfully so! Jesus gave Her to us to be our Mother! Children, who love there earthly mothers, wish that they stay with them as long as they can. Their mothers share the same feeling! Why should it be any different with our Heavenly Mother? Interestingly enough, the messages of all apparitions are the same or similar. As a kind Mother, Gospa warns us and advises us. She speaks about the necessity of prayer, conversion, peace, fasting and the Sacraments. She says nothing new. She only wishes to draw our attention back on what has been forgotten. Many have forgotten to pray with their families during the evening, to fast, to attend Holy Mass on Sundays, to read the Bible... Many live restless lives, argue...

This is what the Catechism of the Catholic Church says about "private" revelations: *Throughout the ages, there have been so-called "private" revelations, some of which have been recognized by the Church. They do not, however, belong to the deposit of faith. It is not their role to improve or complete Christ's definitive Revelation, but to help live more fully by it in a certain period of history. Guided by the Magesterium of the Church, the sensus fidelium knows how to discern and welcome in these revelations whatever constitutes an authentic call of Christ or His saints to the Church (67).*

Christian faith cannot accept "revelations" that claim to surpass or correct the Revelation of which Christ is the fulfilment, as is the case in certain non-Christian religions and also in certain recent sects which base themselves on such "revelations".

Forgiveness is not weakness

All apparitions have one thing in common: forgiveness. It is not easy to forgive but t is necessary. God forgives those who forgive. Not only are those who forgive spiritually healed, they are often physically healed too. How pleasant and joyful one feels after sincerely confessing and making peace with God! One can do anything out of gratitude towards God! After such a confession, many have saved their own lives, their marriages, their families... They have realized that to forgive does not mean to be defeated. It means to be freed from the chains restraining them... Those who have received more are willing to give more too. About the sinful, humble woman who washed His feet Jesus said, "...she wet my feet with her tears and wiped them with her hair..." She has been forgiven much for she loved much (Lk7, 45-47).

The Eucharist – The Christian "Constitution"

Fr. Jozo Zovko's Testimony

Fr. Jozo Zovko was born on the 19th of March 1941, in Uzarići, Parish of Široki Brijeg. He was the eighth of ten children born to Mate and Milka née Gugić. With the start of the Medjugorje apparitions, he was persecuted by the communist government and sentenced to three and a half years of prison. After appealing the sentence, the Federal Court of Belgrade dismissed sections of the indictment and reduced his sentence to a year and six months. In spite of the persecution and pressure by the Yugoslav government, he relentlessly worked with pilgrims from all over the world. Besides holding daily catechetical group sessions for pilgrims, he also held intensive seminars in Tihaljina, Medjugorje and Široki Brijeg.

REMEMBER TO SAY IN PRAYER , "GOD, MAY THY WILL BE DONE."

Welcome dear brothers and sisters! I wish to thank all of you, especially Jakov for his brief, yet clear and beautiful testimony. When he talked about the beginning of the apparitions he reminded me of those difficult times. I did not believe that 10-year-old. Filled with joy and all jubilant, he said that he saw Gospa. He and all the other visionaries were happy yet I was unhappy. Why? I kept asking myself, "What if it is not true? How to avoid a scandal in the parish? What if these six children were put up to this by enemies of the Church or what if they are under the influence of drugs and are telling a lie?" As the parish priest I wanted to protect the faith so I talked to Jakov and the rest of the seers. The conversation I had with them made me sad. They were happy, "exploding" with happiness and joy but only I, at the parish office, was sad. I kept saying to myself, "Lord, if this is not true, what shall happen?" I did not believe them.

This was what it was like in the beginning. There were vineyards all over Medjugorje and now people pray and listen to the word of God here. Today, this here is Mt. Tabor and together we cheer with Peter the Galilean, "It is so nice here Lord. We feel so good in this place. We wish to stay here with You. Mother, we feel happy here. We like the tent You made with your veil, overwhelmed with peace and beauty we feel happy here. " However, Gospa does not wish for us to stop at this. As Her Son did, She also tells us, "Come down, go into the world and be my witnesses!" Peter did not lie about what happened to him at Mt. Tabor. He did not deceive the Church or those to whom he preached in Rome, testifying of what had happened to him at the lake and of other situations he experienced. He talked of what he had seen, heard, touched and experienced. Along with the other apostles, Peter was a living witness. He did not make Jesus, His preaching and miracles up. He merely conveyed what he saw, heard and experienced.

Jakov is also not inventing anything. Like Peter, the other seers and him spoke of what they saw and heard. How can we not accept their testimonies when Gospa did everything in order for our hearts to be at ease today, for the words of the visionaries to fall on fertile ground; like balm to a wound? It is truly nice here.

While I was touching our Mother's veil, I thought of the doctor whom the police forced to say to the children, "Put my hand on Gospa's veil. I also want to see Gospa like you." "Why not! Let's do it," said the boy, Jakov. He took her hand and put in on Gospa's veil. After the doctor pulled her hand back, a stain appeared on the veil. Jakov and the rest of the seers started to cry. The doctor asked them why they were crying and they said, "You made Her veil dirty." "How?" asked the doctor and the visionaries explained that a stain appeared where her hand on Gospa's veil was. The doctor was left speechless and the children continued to cry.

During the following days, the doctor could not sleep. She called me and asked if she could come talk to me about what the children had said concerning Gospa's veil, for it was occupying her thoughts. She asked me what to do and I told her, "You need to cleanse yourself." She did, through the Sacrament of Reconciliation.

Her life with God and Gospa had begun and, ever since, she testifies of Gospa's great doings.

Medjugorje is not a place of deceit, delusion, fraud or fantasy. Many merciful events took place proving this. There is not much to say. Kneel, open up and show your weaknesses and wounds, bring all your sins and say, "Wash me, Jesus, in Your blood!" Gospa relentlessly encourages us to do so. She tells us to cleanse our souls through the Sacrament of Confession at least once a month.

Our Mother arrived in tears and talked of the Eucharist. The Eucharist can be compared to the story of Gospa's visit to her cousin Elizabeth. Elizabeth said cheerfully, "The Mother of my God has come to me." As Elizabeth recognized in her heart who had come to visit her, so can every Christian feel the power of the Eucharist. The first chalice, the first tabernacle, the first cathedral and shrine – Her name is the Queen of Peace, Her name is the Immaculate Virgin.

The children did not see something that was a fruit of their imagination or illness here. No, they saw what John the Apostle saw and described in the twelfth chapter of the Apocalypse: a woman clothed with the sun and upon Her head a crown of twelve stars, a woman being with child by the name of Jesus, giving birth to Him and giving Him to all of us. This is the woman who is appearing to theses visionaries all these years. These young people are Her witnesses and, like the first Christians, they wish to convey this joyful news to every man. As the first Christians did not lose hope and give way to pressure, despite persecution, testifying, "Our Jesus is our God and Lord, we know who we adore and worship," so do the visionaries unflaggingly convey our Mother's messages.

Jesus teaches us to judge everything by its fruits. Confessors and those who have healed from Satan's poisonous bite are witnesses to this. It is in this place that many have rejected the use of drugs, abandoned their lustful and adulterous lives and have accepted Jesus. In Medjugorje, millions of people have experienced mass as a sacrament of love, dedication and return to God while the Church is experienced in its true sense. Therefore, to me, Medjugorje is a phenomenon which completely coincides with the Revelation; nothing contrary to the Church's teachings is going on there.

For this reason, I view Medjugorje in the light of the Bible. If we look at Chapter 13 of Luke's Gospel we can read about Jesus' parable of the Lost Sheep – about a shepherd who had a hundred sheep. When the shepherd lost one of his sheep he was sad and restless. Why? He knew her; she had a name and he could not forget about her. Therefore, he needed to find her and find out what had happened to her. He surely asked himself, "Why was I so careless and did not watch over them?

Why did I not count them and keep them together?" He left everything to go find his lost sheep. When he found it, he lifted it and, running, carried it back on his shoulders. He was happy and at ease because he had all his sheep together again.

There is a similar parable, about a woman who lost a drachma, a coin. Not only was she even more destitute when she lost it but she also asked herself how it could have happened and why was she so careless. She became very restless so she decided to look for it. When she found the coin, she shared her joy with her neighbours. She invited them to celebrate with her because all had ended well. Then there is a third parable: a father lost his son and became miserable. He felt as if he lost everything and had nothing anymore. He did everything he could to feel happiness again. The son, who was also far from his father, had also lost everything but one thing – an experience: "My father is kind and loving. He is even kind to his servants. Me? I sleep and eat with pigs and I am completely humiliated. I shall return to my father even if it means that I shall become a servant. Nevertheless, I shall be content at the sight of his loving face." So, the prodigal son returned and was embraced by his father. What a reunion! What a new beginning! What grace! What reconciliation! Both son and father cried. The father dressed his son in his best robes and ordered the servants to prepare a feast – let there be celebration, singing and joy! The older brother asked, "Why? Father, why such joy?" His father replied, "There was a grave in my soul; my son was dead and now he is alive. He was lost but now is back in my arms again. Rejoice too my son!"

These parables excellently reflect our daily lives. We all have lost something. In a world in which Satan's deeds are rising – terrorism, hatred and violence – everything priests, bishops and the Pope warns of, as well as what Gospa speaks of in Her messages, mankind has lost true peace. However, our Mother teaches us how to restore this peace – only through fasting and prayer. This weapon was entrusted to us by Jesus and the Church fosters it from the very beginning. Gospa clearly said, "If you wish to become peacekeepers, you must first find the drachmae of peace within your hearts." This is possible by fasting and through sincere prayer.

Precisely this is happening in Medjugorje during all these years. By taking a look at Apparition Hill and Cross Mountain one can find proof of this. Every single rock on both hill and mountain is abraded by the bear feet of pilgrims in search of God's blessing through our Heavenly Mother's intercession. The rocks were abraded by the steps of peacekeepers; apostles of peace who have found the most valuable drachmae.

Gospa repeats in Medjugorje what our crucified Jesus said to Saint Francis of Assisi, "Francis, the Church is not doing well, it is falling into ruins." "Lord, how can I help You? What do You wish me to do?" "Help me rebuild the Church!" The young man replied, "Yes, Lord, I am ready to do anything for You!" He took the Bible and opened it three times. All three times Jesus said to him, "Leave everything for you have me! I am your teacher, your peace and your joy." Francis succeeded and became the Great King's messenger.

Brothers, Gospa invites us by saying, "You might have come from ruined families but you yourselves will not have ruined families." We heard Jakov say that the youth of today easily gives in into shallow pleasures as this is a time during which the cult of hedonism prevails." Misguided young people sell their bodies on stages throughout the world thinking that it is ideal, trendy and modern. Our Mother says that this is not the path to peace. It is the exact opposite – a path to restlessness, a path which leads to the demise of civilization, morality, family and the world in whole.

How to find the drachmae and the lost son? How to find peace in marriage and achieve holiness of family, priesthood and monastic life? There are no quick and cheap solutions or effective tricks. The only way to achieve this is to walk with our Mother and to listen to Her advice. She calls us to Blessed Pope John Paul's II "constitution" of peace, which is the Holy Eucharist. We need to place Holy Mass at the centre of our lives and love it with all our hearts. We were overjoyed when, headed by the Pope, we heard the calls of the Italian bishops from Bari. They said, "We cannot survive without Sundays, without Holy Mass. We need the Eucharist!" Young people, you do not need disco bars for they have disappointed and blinded you. You need to meet with our Risen Christ and His Mother. You need the day of the Lord when you can devote yourselves to prayer and reflect upon God's deeds of salvation.

In accordance with Gospa's wish, Medjugorje has found its home in millions of hearts. Today, the entire world is in Medjugorje – people from all parts of the world are here. This is confirmation that the work of God is taking place and that we are becoming one family – One Church. The Church is born at the altar, from the Eucharist. It is blessed and renewed by the Eucharist.

Pilgrims, when you return home, do not forget Cross Mountain, which you have experienced as your Mt. Tabor. May the flame you found, the new light, fulfil your hearts and may it remove all the darkness and impurities from your souls. When you return home, do not go back to your old lives! Become new witnesses just like our visionaries and millions of other pilgrims have.

We need to rebuild our lives. How? Take Gospa's advice and start your day with short but fervent prayers. This does not mean that you do not have to pray the Rosary or other prayers. However, short but fervent prayers during difficult times (when we are travelling through the spiritual desert, when we are restless, when sins are burdening and attacking us) can lift us and give us strength to endure and to recognise God's will. On your way to work, in your car, at school, at the hospital, during temptation and trouble, direct your sincere and fervent prayers to our Lord and He shall surely invigorate you. Remember and think of how St. Francis deeply prayed all night, having only one sentence in his mind, "My God and my everything!"

The terror of the communist regime, the difficult and dangerous times during 1981 forced Fr. Jozo Zovko to think about where to hide his confidential material in order to keep them from being destroyed. Several days preceding his arrest (he was arrested on the 17th of August 1981, at 11 PM) he called Ivan Vasilj – Ića and entrusted him with the tape-recordings he made of the visionaries.

Ivan Vasilj - Iće Grgasović with his son Mario on the occasion of consecrating a statue of the Queen of Peace, as of 9th September 2001

"My God and my everything!"

St. Francis

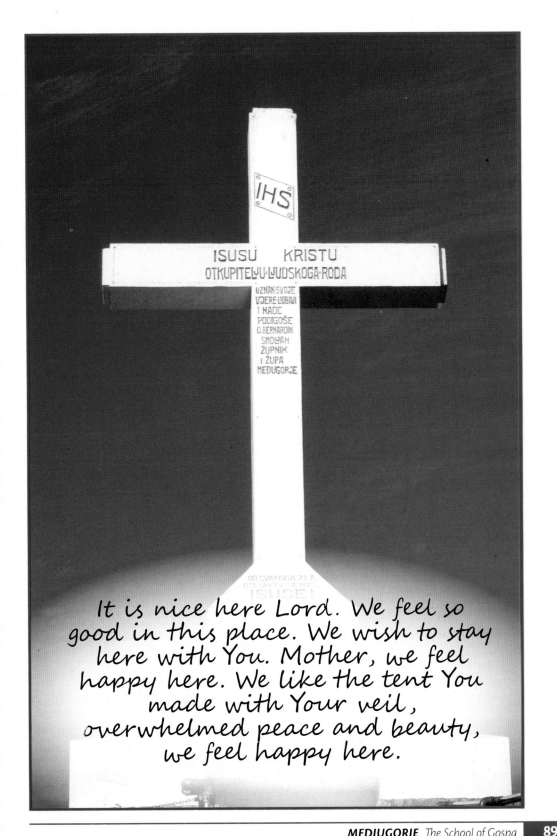

It is nice here Lord. We feel so good in this place. We wish to stay here with You. Mother, we feel happy here. We like the tent You made with Your veil, overwhelmed peace and beauty, we feel happy here.

*Gospa of Medjugorje – The Queen of Peace, by Italian artist and sculptor Carmelo Puzzola
(on display at the Parish Office of Medjugorje)*

God is Powerful and Merciful
Fr. Petar Ljubičić's Testimony

Fr. Petar was born in Prisoje (christened in Podhum near Livno) on the 28th October 1946, as the first of ten children. He completed elementary school in Prisoje. Ever since he was a small child, he felt the call to follow Jesus. Till this day it is a mystery as to why the calling came so early on. The secret may lay in the fact that his mother did not have children during the first few years of marriage. She vowed to God that she would give birth to as many children as He wishes and that she would consecrate them all to Him. God fulfilled her sincere prayer and she gave birth to ten children and already has thirty grandchildren as well as twenty great-grandchildren.

In autumn, Petar Ljubučić left for the seminary in Zadar. He then moved to Split and graduated in Dubrovnik in 1967. On the 15th of July he put the Franciscan robe on and started his one-year novitiate service in Humac. He studied philosophy and theology in Sarajevo in 1968 and continued his studies in Königsten (Taunus) in Germany. He received the Holy Order on the 29th of June, 1972, in Königstein and completed his studies the following year. As a priest he served in the following parishes: Vitina – five years, Tihaljina – four years, Seonice – two years, Medjugorje – ten and a half years. In February of 1995, he left for Switzerland and became a missionary priest for the Croatians in Zurich where he remained for three and a half years. In August of 1998, he served as a missionary priest in Ticino (Switzerland). From the 3rd of March 2000, he served in Hosenfeld in Germany where he stayed until the 15th of November 2008, when he transferred to Bukovica to serve as chaplain and remains there to this day.

TO PRAY WITH THE HEART MEANS TO PRAY DEVOUTLY.

I greet you all with great joy and love, dear pilgrims. You have received great grace and a gift by being here in this holy place where Gospa appears. Since the first day of the apparition till today, rivers of pilgrims come here to this merciful place. Everybody wonders what attracts so many pilgrims here and the answer is: our Heavenly Mother.

Gospa often appears during times of difficulty for Christ's Church and mankind. If we look back in history, Gospa appeared in Lourdes when the Church was threatened by Freemasons. She appeared in Fatima when godlessness started to take over. Gospa appeared in Medjugorje during difficult times of communism.

Our Heavenly Mother came to prompt us to strengthen our faith and belief in God. As She Herself said, She came to wake our faith up. On the first day, She appeared with Her Son Jesus in Her arms. Through this act She conveyed to us that She brings Her Son Jesus to us so that we may have peace, joy and happiness in Him – everything the heart yearns for. Everybody wishes to be happy, free. Everybody wishes to possess perfect peace. However, Gospa said, "Peace can only be achieved through strong faith and conversion, as well as through penance, fasting and praying with the heart."

Conversion is a grace, a gift. It is a grace to recognise your own sins and change your way of life. A Scottish doctor, who invented some types of medication and medical appliances, was asked by his student which one of his inventions did he deem most important and the doctor replied, "My greatest discovery is the realization that I am a sinner and that Jesus is my saviour." The first step towards conversion is the realization that we are sinners. To convert means to stop sinning and to live as God's children. To convert means to be fulfilled by Jesus Christ as St. Paul was and to leave everything and renew ourselves out of love for God. This grace is given here to everyone.

A young man from Napoli came to Medjugorje. He was a drug addict and had committed sins against all of God's Commandments. As the Italian saying goes, he had a 'bag full of sins'. Praying before Gospa's statue in Medjugorje he said, "Gospa, I heard that You are appearing here in Medjugorje and that your Son has helped many people. I am a sinner and I shall give Jesus a chance and let Him help me. I cannot live like this anymore. I tried to commit suicide three times. I searched for happiness in all the wrong places and did not find any. Please, Gospa, help me! If You do, I will end my wrong-doings right here."

Gospa did help him. By his own testimony, he was unconscious for two or three minutes and then a thought to confess came into his mind. He wondered how he could find an Italian priest to whom he could confess to. Gospa had already taken care of that and he went to confession. The following is the young man's testimony:

"I will never forget that half hour I spent in the confessional. The priest was patient and listened to me. I told him my every sin. I had a feeling that Jesus was telling me that it was alright, that He had forgiven me and that I can carry on confessing." The young man testifies that Christians are not aware how great the gift of Holy Confession is and how it is an important Sacrament. "It is a psychoanalysis of ourselves, it is our cure, our resurrection. With every grave sin we commit, we kill God within us and we kill ourselves spiritually. When God forgives us our sins and when we repent, we rise and become new beings. I have become indescribably joyful and I return to Medjugorje every year to thank Mary for the graces I have received. Other young people, who know how I had lived before and know how I live now, come with me."

This is a conversion you have witnessed here. Realization of your sins always precedes confession. It is always a gift from God. We are powerless but God is therefore powerful. If we allow Him, He can make righteous men and saints of us.

I served in the Parish of Medjugorje for ten and a half years and I have met with tens of thousands of pilgrims. None of these pilgrims ever told me that their lives are wonderful and that they do not have any difficulties. People I met throughout the world have told me about their problems, their illnesses and so on. Hearing all this I concluded that God allows all of this so that we may seek Him and meet with Him. After being banished from paradise, man seeks for his true place. However, spiritual cleansing is necessary for this to be achieved. Our life on earth is a time of conversion, grace and prayer, a time to decide for God. Therefore, choose Jesus, live with Him and then your paradise on earth shall commence.

God has performed miracles in Medjugorje. A nun, who often comes to Medjugorje with pilgrims, says that the greatest gift one can receive in Medjugorje is to convert and become a new person. Many priests told me that they themselves have been reborn in Medjugorje. They say that in Medjugorje there faith has evolved, that their faith in Jesus' presence in the Holy Eucharist has strengthened. A priest from Manama comes to Medjugorje every year and says that the peace and happiness he finds here cannot be found elsewhere. He says that he lives by the messages Gospa leaves for us here and that he preaches about them. They are the messages of the Gospel.

Was it not Jesus who said in the Gospel, "Convert and believe in the Gospel! Pray and fast!" We become new people when we do this. Although man has crosses and burdens to bear, he is lucky to have Jesus as an example. Through his suffering and resurrection, Jesus showed us that we can endure anything. Jesus gives us strength.

He has enough holy blood to wash mankind's sins; all of them. He is so powerful that he gives every person the ability to resurrect. Therefore, it is worthwhile to live, pray and sacrifice for our future is then secured.

Eternal happiness and bliss awaits us but we need to believe completely, without a doubt. I wish for all of us to become participants of Jesus' victory.

Two ladies took a walk down the street and talked with each other. One of them said to the other that she finds it difficult to understand resurrection and asked how it was possible. Her friend answered her by saying, "I don't find it a problem. I believe in Jesus Christ. He came to us and lived a short time and then he was sentenced to death. He died for me and my sins. On the third day, he rose from the dead. I believe what he said that someday we all shall all rise. He said, 'I am the resurrection and the life. He who believes in me will live, even though he dies.' This is enough for me. I look forward to eternal life. Dear sister, I shall pray that you also believe in this. I would be very sad not to see you in Paradise once when I get there. Therefore, believe. If you think it is not possible then say: Jesus, you have resurrected, I wish to believe that You shall grant me this grace too."

Did Jesus not raise Lazarus, who spent four days in the grave, from the dead? God is the Master of life and death. Jesus raised the young man from Nain as well as Jairus' daughter. If He was able to raise them, He can raise us too. This is a great grace – a gift of faith. Therefore, we should pray never to doubt. Many have found their faith here. Recently, when I attended a spiritual seminar for exorcists, I spoke of God and His deeds in Medjugorje. After the lecture, a woman approached me and said that she would never forget Medjugorje, "When I came to Medjugorje with my family, we all converted. Now, we are a new family. We attend Holy Mass, we read the Bible each day and we look forward to our Lord's day. We feel as if we are in Heaven. We overcome every problem by praying the Rosary. Whenever I see someone heavily burdened with problems in life, I tell him or her to go to Medjugorje to receive strength from the fountain of grace."

Another woman phoned me and told me how happy she had been ever since she started believing in Jesus Christ for she now knows why she suffers, who she lives for and to whom she prays. She is happy to meet with Jesus soon and to always be with Him yet she is sad, for many do not know Jesus Christ. So little is needed to meet with Jesus Christ, the source of eternal happiness. The woman also told me that she prays for people to convert.

These are the gifts God gives to people. Therefore, we should all carry this message of grace. It is important that God can depend on us and that He loves us.

Andreas is a young man from Prague. His father ensured his education in the USA, yet he did not receive the most important thing from his father. This is what he says, "I was not raised in faith. My life was empty and I did not feel like either studying or working. I simply never knew my purpose. I came to Medjugorje and discovered Jesus Christ to be the purpose of life. I am forever thankful to God for the graces He bestowed upon me." God is truly almighty and merciful. Prayer from the heart is most important for it means to pray devoutly. If I have sinned gravely, my prayer does not go very far and God cannot hear and answer my prayer for there is something blocking the path between God and me. This is why I must cleanse myself from grave sin through confession. If we are in a situation where we cannot confess before a priest then it is necessary to truly repent; penance which comes out of love. For instance, we can say, "God, I have sinned. I deserve to go to hell for my sins. I am not sorry for deserving hell but I am sorry for offending You, true Love, and therefore I repent. Please forgive me!" This is an example of perfect penance after which God shall immediately forgive you for your sins. I advise you to confess whenever you have the opportunity. This is how you receive God's grace.

Do not forget to pray, "God, may Thy will be done." Gospa, our Mother taught us this when the angel Gabriel appeared to Her. She immediately accepted the will of God and a miracle took place. Through the power of the Holy Spirit, Gospa carried Jesus under Her heart. Our prayers are also answered if we accept God's will. What is God's will? It means to accept Jesus Christ, who was crucified then died and resurrected for all of us. We need to force our way through this difficult life and know that we are going to God. It is God's will that we open our hearts and give them to Him so that He may heal and save them. This is great grace. You cannot wish for greater happiness than of the one God can give you. Surrender to God's will and He will make you happy.

A German lady was ill with multiple sclerosis while her husband was ill with cancer. She had a son whose girlfriend was pregnant and wanted an abortion. This poor woman had a heavy cross to carry. However, she came to Medjugorje and prayed in the church, "Gospa, I know that you love me and I love you. Please help me. Pray for me and with me so that God's will concerning my husband and my son's girlfriend, who is carrying a baby, may be done. I know that God is kind to those who pray to Him and love Him. May God's will concerning me too be done. May God give me the strength I need to carry this cross." At that very moment, she heard a voice saying, "Stand up, you are cured!" The woman got up and went to the chapel to thank Jesus. When she returned home, her husband was waiting for her by the door and told her that the doctors revealed to him that he was free of cancer. The next day, her son and his girlfriend came over to see her. They announced to her that they were going to get married in a Catholic church and that they were going to keep the baby. Three miracles occurred because of the faith this woman had!

Recently, a young man from Italy came to Medjugorje and, in a conversation with a priest, he said, "My parents are divorced and I did not find love within my family. I looked for love outside of my home but found evil instead. I kept bad company. They used drugs and soon I too became a drug addict. I even started stealing in order to raise money for drugs. Once I stole a large amount of diamonds. I heard a woman was organizing a pilgrimage to Medjugorje so I decided to join the pilgrimage. I wanted to cash the stolen diamonds here in Medjugorje. While I was climbing Apparition Hill, I kept asking myself to whom I could sell these diamonds to.

While I was standing and looking at the statue of Gospa, I heard Her speak to me, She said, "Leave that. Do not do what you are planning on doing!"

I thought to myself that by speaking to me Gospa was trying to hinder my plans. I went back to the church and kept thinking of the words I heard. Deep in thought, I came across a woman who was begging. As soon as I saw her I decided to give her the stolen diamonds and I did. The woman was surprised and overjoyed. The diamonds must have been worth ten to fifteen thousand euros.

The next step was to go to Holy Confession. I experienced an amazing confession. I confessed all my sins to the Lord. I had committed many grave sins by the time I turned eighteen. I could not fall asleep without taking sleeping pills. Ever since my confession, Jesus freed me from my addiction to pills. I am the happiest man on earth now and money is no longer important to me. The peace I have in my heart now is important. This is treasure." This is how Gospa helps Her children here in Medjugorje.

Recently, I heard that a girl born in Padova, close to the Basilica of St. Anthony, was cured of muscle dystrophy in Medjugorje. At the age of sixteen, she dreamt of having a big career someday. She explains how her symptoms started, "I had a high fever for three days and felt that I was loosing strength in my legs. I was diagnosed with dystrophy and was wheelchair-bound. All my plans fell apart and I dreaded life in a wheelchair. On the 24th of June, 2005, I came to Medjugorje and that is when my life changed. We went to Apparition Hill. I was carried up the hill and was told that Ivan was going to have an apparition. I prayed, not for myself but for people who had more serious illnesses than mine was.

Before the apparition took place, our guide said, 'Gospa will come here soon. If we ask Her for something with deep faith, She will convey our wishes to Her Son and He will answer our prayers.' I listened to the guide with disbelief. I did not pray to be healed as I thought it was too much to ask for and that it was impossible. I prayed to God to give me strength to accept my life in a wheelchair and to make my life a little easier and a more fulfilled. The apparition lasted for five or six minutes. During the apparition I saw a light. I did not see Gospa but I felt Her presence. Deep within, I felt Her as my Mother, I felt Her love for me and Her wish to help me. When the apparition was over, the light disappeared and I started to get up but then I fell. I hit my head against a rock and everyone thought I was dead. However, I got up again because Jesus had healed me. It was truly a great miracle. Yet, for me, the greatest miracle was my experience of faith. I felt God there. I felt His love for us. He sent His loving Mother to us. He calls for us to convert. Conversion is like a fire, it keeps the flame of the Eucharist and prayer burning. Prayer solves all our problems." Today, this girl testifies of God's power and presence throughout the world, especially in Medjugorje.

In the Italian part of Switzerland, a girl entered a convent of an enclosed type. According to her testimony, when she came to Medjugorje for the first time she felt the presence of Gospa. She felt as if every rock in Medjugorje was telling her that Gospa was there. She cried when she spoke with Mirjana and Vicka . She was thankful for the grace she received to be able to talk with the visionaries who see Gospa. Then she asked Jesus, "Jesus, You did everything for me. You died and rose for me. What do you expect of me?" A few days later, Jesus said, "I want you to be my bride." It was then when she made her decision to become a nun. She lives and prays in a convent of an enclosed type, joyful to be close to God. She says that she is in Medjugorje in spirit everyday and that she prays for all pilgrims.

Gospa appears everyday and loves us. It is Her wish that we all come to Her with the gift of holiness. Many people ask me about the secrets. All I can say is this: Mirjana has received ten secrets. Each secret will be revealed ten days before it occurs and we shall know where and how it will happen. Seven days before the secret is revealed, a priest will have to fast and pray with Mirjana. The first two secrets are warnings. They will be proof that the visionaries were telling the truth. The third secret is about a secret sign which will appear on Apparition Hill. Those who have believed and were here will feel joy because of this. It will also be a calling to everyone to convert and start believing. This is all I can say about the secrets for now. Gospa always warns us to be ready. Do not be afraid of anything! Celebrate God with your lives! Be brothers and sisters, help one another and do not make the lives of others difficult! In this way we will surely walk towards happiness and bliss.

I celebrate You, Jesus Christ, along with all these pilgrims. Lay Your hands on each of them. You know their needs and answer their prayers. Heal their souls and bodies. Jesus, give them strength to always do good. Give them grace to grow in faith, hope and love so that they may all come to Paradise. By the intercession of our Heavenly Mother and all saints, may you be blessed, body and soul be healed and saved, by Almighty God, the Father, The Son and the Holy Spirit. Amen!

You have received grace to
be in this holy place where
Gospa appears today.

Gospa always warns us to
be ready. Do not fear
anything! Celebrate God
with your life!

What do we know about the secrets?
The revealing of the secrets will come as consolation and joy for all
Fr. Petar Ljubičić

Fr. Petar became known when seer Mirjana chose him to reveal the secrets Gospa confided to her. Mirjana has received all ten secrets. When the time for the revealing of each secret comes, Mirjana will reveal each secret to Fr. Petar ten days before each secret is to take place. When each secret is revealed to him, he shall fast and pray for seven days. Three days before the realization of each secret, he will be allowed to reveal the secret to all.

• *Fr. Petar, the seer Mirjana chose you to reveal the ten secrets Gospa confided to her. How did you receive this news? Are you honoured or do you feel a little fear?*

Fr. Petar: One night, almost thirty years ago, in Medjugorje, a few people told me that visionary Mirjana had chosen me to reveal the secrets. I thought that someone was joking with me. I told the visionaries that these were serious matters and were not to be played with...

I was in deep thought a few days later and said to myself, "What if it's true?" I did not feel at ease. For her to choose me was also some kind of small secret. It is truly a great honour but also a responsibility. I did not feel afraid at all.

When I saw Mirjana, she said to me, "Do you already know that you are going to reveal the secrets to the world when the time comes?!"

"Is it possible?!" I replied, short of breath. It is difficult to describe in words what I felt and went through. I felt great joy and I felt secure...

• *What can you tell us about the secrets, about their content? What do they say? When will the time to reveal them come?*

Fr. Petar: They are of a confidential nature – as the word secret implies. I do not know their content. I can say that the secrets refer to special events which are going to take place at a specific time and in a specific place. I do not know when this will be. I am sure they are closer each day.

The message of each secret could be: our lives and the time we live in are gifts from God. These gifts need to be utilized by relentlessly working on being saved! We should not live as if we are never going to answer for the way we live and for the things we do! Above all, it is important to be ready to meet with our inner and our living God at any moment! If we live this way, we have nothing to fear and we do not need to ask ourselves what is going to happen. This is how we will be ready.

• *You will reveal all ten secrets. How are you going to reveal them? What is the secret concerning the visible and permanent sign, which Gospa promised to leave, about?*

Fr. Petar: When the time to reveal the first secret comes, Mirjana will give me something resembling a parchment. Its size is the size of an A4 paper. Mirjana received this from Gospa so that she could know when each secret will be realized. All of the secrets are written on it. I will only be able to read the first secret. As one secret is realized, I will only be able to read the following secret, not all of them. Then I will fast and pray for seven days. Three days before the secret is realized, I will be allowed to disclose it to everyone. I will reveal what exactly will happen, where it will happen, the time when it will occur and for how long it will be happening!

Mirjana said that the first two secrets concern Medjugorje and that they will be about a great warning. Gospa came to a small village called Bijakovići, in the Parish of Medjugorje, and has been appearing there for thirty years. When these two secrets are revealed, everyone will know that the visionaries were telling the truth and that the apparitions are authentic.

The third secret concerns a visible sign on Apparition Hill. It will be perceived as great joy on the part of those who accepted the apparitions as a gift from Heaven and the Queen of Peace. It will be a sign for many to convert and return to God.

We must not forget that this is the time of conversion and prayer, a time to choose God. It is not wise to wait for the sign for it could be too late then.

• *What could take place after the revealing of the first secrets? What future awaits Medjugorje?*

Fr. Petar: Gospa has repeated for many times that this is a time of grace – a time for prayer, conversion, spiritual cleansing and a time to choose God. Every moment of our life is very important and therefore we have to use these moments. By devoting ourselves completely to God in prayer we bless every moment of our life. This will fill us with joy and we will be able to bear the burden of life with more ease.

I believe that when the secrets are revealed they will help us become more serious and more responsible and that sincere conversion will become our life goal. There will surely be miraculous signs and great conversions. All conversions, as well as spiritual and bodily healings that have occurred until now, are proof that Heaven has opened above Medjugorje and that the Queen of Peace has come and has stayed with us for so long. For Her to stay as long as She has in Medjugorje is a rare occurrence if we look back in the history of mankind.

The revealing of the secrets will come as consolation and joy for all. All those who have believed and have tried to live as believers by Jesus' Gospel will be joyful. We witness how many pilgrims come to the Queen of Peace in Medjugorje each year. When the secrets start being revealed, even more will come. Those who have been uninterested in the events will also surely wake up.

The future of Medjugorje is good. It will serve as a spiritual magnet attracting everyone even more.

• *The emotional conversions and miraculous healings are proof that the apparitions are authentic (true). Will the revealing of the secrets be crucial for the approval of the Medjugorje apparitions by the Church?*

Fr. Petar: It is my deep belief that the Medjugorje apparitions already have convincing proof of authenticity. Among a few other conditions, only two miraculous healings, scientifically proven, are enough for the approval of supernatural apparitions.

With the help of many pilgrims in Medjugorje, I have described my experiences in two books: The Call of the Queen of Peace and This Is the Time of Grace. During my time abroad, I met people who told me that they could not imagine their lives without the Queen of Peace and the graces they experienced while in Medjugorje. People were cured of different, severe and medically incurable illnesses. This is proof that God, through Mary's intercession is at work here.

You are right, the revealing of the secrets will be crucial for the Church's approval of these apparitions.

• *Considering the time and place of Gospa's apparitions, can one state that there is a link between the events in Medjugorje and the historical events which took place in Europe and former Yugoslavia thereafter?*

Fr. Petar: Of course there is! Gospa's apparition in Medjugorje is not accidental. On the 19th of January 1982, one of the visionaries said to me that Gospa told her that communism will fall, that there will be war and that Croatia will be free. She invited us to pray so as to minimize the upcoming tragedies.

Unfortunately, we did not completely accept the call for prayer and conversion and for this reason we had to pay our freedom with a great number of casualties. If we had listened to our heavenly Mother, things would have probably been different. Those who say that Gospa appears to them would surely not play with such a serious matter. The visionaries were submitted to very strict scientific examinations on a number of occasions and the conclusion was that they were not lying.

If a person, who is physically and psychologically healthy, says that during prayer he or she experiences something, it is upon us to grant this person our trust. Of course, by their own conscience, everyone is free to accept or refuse this. Besides the above mentioned, taking into consideration the many fruits of Medjugorje, it is clear that this all is the work of God. All those who do not believe in the authenticity of the apparitions have not contributed to anybody's conversion and growth in faith.

• *Why has Gospa been appearing so often in the last one-hundred and fifty years? What is happening to mankind that so many interventions by Heaven are needed?*

Fr. Petar: The history of the apparitions show that Gospa always appeared to people before the onset of great and disastrous events. If we take into consideration the last one-hundred and fifty years, we can see how our heavenly Mother expressed Her love and care for people through appearing. She tried to prevent the worst through these apparitions and messages.

For example, Gospa appeared in Lourdes in 1858, during the time when France and Europe were threatened by moral liberalism and masonry. Something similar occurred in 1917, in Portugal, when the atheist-communist monster threatened the world with terrible grievances. She also appeared to visionaries ten years before the horrific murders in Ruanda where, according to some, a million and a half people were killed. As a caring Mother, Gospa tried to warn Her children of the great dangers ahead. She tried to show them a way out and give them the help they were in need of.

This is what happened when She first appeared in Medjugorje on the 24th of June, 1981. Gospa appeared ten years before the brutal war in Croatia and Bosnia and Herzegovina broke out. Gospa appeared in Medjugorje with baby Jesus, true God and true man, in Her arms. This is Her message, Her gift and Her help for today's world. There is nothing greater or more important that Gospa could have given to us. Jesus is our greatest and most important gift.

• *How would you describe today's world? Why is it so chaotic and so full of crisis?*

Fr. Petar: Everybody is aware that the state of the world today is chaotic, critical and difficult. We are all witnesses to this and we can all agree upon the following: man has never been less sure and more anxious, worried and unhappy, sinful and ill. Man has never been in more trouble and has never suffered more than he does today... The world is in trouble and in crisis. This is the least that can be said. The crisis experienced in the world does not mean its downfall. However, it is also not ruled out. Crisis is, first of all, an opportunity. If this opportunity is not seized then it can turn into destruction which can be general and take on great proportions and terrible forms.

The problem lies in the fact that people wish to fix injustice with injustice, war with war, family problems with divorce, addiction with addiction. Addicts are given smaller dosages of heroin to keep them away from large dosages; they are given less dangerous drugs to keep them from more dangerous ones. People do not see that they are putting out a fire with a flame, or maybe they see but are impotent in lack of something better and more successful.

Many speak of freedom today. Yes, freedom is a gift from God to man. Through freedom man can choose goodness and achieve it. This is called responsible freedom. This gift must not be abused as some do by destroying families, all things valuable as well as humane virtues. Some go too far and insult everything sacred and use profane language. Where does all this lead to? It leads to a small hell in this valley of tears. Is it not still clear to some that man cannot and must not be without God? Without God, man becomes unhappy, empty, hopeless and a slave of his own sinful requests. He simply does not know how to be happy without God. It is so unfortunate that today's modern man does not understand this. Here lies the main reason to all troubles and sufferings, terrors and fears, to everything that takes place around us today.

• *Is Medjugorje a continuance of Fatima? If you think so, can you explain how?*

Fr. Petar: A good answer to this question was given by an Italian priest, Fr. Primo Martinuzzi. As a physician, he participated in the examinations of the visionaries. It had such an impact on him that he started thinking about changing his calling even though he had been engaged and was getting ready for marriage at the time. In agreement with his fiancé, in 1985, he left his vocation as a doctor and went on to study theology. He was ordained in 1991. This is what he said, "Medjugorje entered my life as soon as I heard of the apparitions. I believed in it, accepted it and started conveying the messages to priests and bishops I would meet. I cannot imagine my life and work as a priest if I had not learned of Medjugorje. I share the opinion of some theologists and Maryologists who view Medjugorje as a fulfillment of Lourdes and Fatima. After years of temptation and suffering, I am positive that the time for the return of many prodigal sons will come. They will especially seek our priests and say that they wish to meet Jesus and that they need Mary. He says that Medjugorje prepared this time for the great return to God. I agree with him.

Gospa appeared to innocent shepherds Lucia, Jacinta and Francisco who were the children of destitute but religious parents from Fatima in Portugal. A woman in white appeared to the children and, in a motherly manner, called them and said, "Sin is a great evil, it is the cause of all other evils. People need to change and pray for the forgiveness of their sins. They must not insult our Lord who has already been insulted enough!"

The Blessed Virgin said to the children, as well as to us, "Pray, pray a lot and sacrifice yourselves for sinners. Many souls are going to hell for there is no one to sacrifice themselves and pray for them."

According to those who see and talk with Her, Gospa of Medjugorje – the Queen of Peace, says something very similar.

• *Fr. Petar, do you feel that our heavenly Mother has especially rewarded our Croatian nation? And, in conclusion, what do you wish to say to the readers in connection with the 30th anniversary of Gospa's apparitions (what is your message at this time)?*

Fr. Petar: Awaiting the anniversary of Gospa's apparitions (25th of June 2011 – 10,955 days) I ask myself: Why did our dear Croatian nation, that has suffered so much, receive such an exceptional grace – the gift of the apparitions of the Queen of Peace. As a nation, we should be proud that Heaven had such mercy and we should be thankful for all the graces we have received during this time. Our nation's history was a turbulent and difficult one. We suffered, not for years but for centuries.

Heaven could not stay silent anymore. It parted and Gospa came. She relentlessly repeats, "Dear children, I am your Mother and I love you. I see that you are troubled and can not find a way out. I am here to help you and lead you to my Son Jesus in whom you will find the sense and purpose of your life. He is your joy and tranquility, your happiness and salvation! Have strong faith in God and pray to Him. Convert and fast! Be worthy of your Christianity!"

What else can I say to the readers except to repeat what Gospa has been telling us for thirty years. Be thankful to God! He is our loving Father. He expects us to realize the plans He has for each of us. His plan, or better yet, His holy will, is that we love Him too and that we always count on His blessing in order to live joyfully and, in the end, to arrive safely in the port of eternal salvation.

His work in this difficult and turbulent time is visible. We must make use this time of grace He gives us. We must be brave and completely surrender ourselves to Him. If we do so, we will turn each moment of our lives into moments of salvation, for ourselves as well as for our brothers and sisters. What is more beautiful and more sacred than that?!

Cross Mountain
A place where God's nation gathers

Cross Mountain overlooks Medjugorje (520 m above sea level). On the 15th Of March 1934, parishioners built an 8, 56 m high reinforced concrete cross with the following words engraved on the cross, "To Jesus Christ, the Redeemer of the Human Race, as a sign of faith, love and hope, in memory of the 1900th anniversary of the Passion of Jesus."

A relic of the authentic cross of Jesus, which especially arrived from Rome for this occasion, was embedded in the centre of the cross. Ever since, Holy Mass is celebrated at its base on the first Sunday after the Nativity of the Virgin Mary, in honor of the Feast of the Exaltation of the Holy Cross. By testimony of the visionaries, in the message of the 30th of August, 1984, Gospa said,

"Dear children,
the cross was also in God's plan when you built it.
These days especially, climb the mountain and pray before the cross.
I am in need of your prayers.
Thank you for having responded to my call!"

Since the apparitions started in 1981, Cross Mountain has become a place where God and people from all over the world meet. The Way of the Cross has been prayed on Cross Mountain ever since the apparitions began. In the beginning, the stations were marked with wooden crosses and in 1988 bronze plaques were erected and put in their place. The plaques are the work of Italian artist and sculptor Carmelo Puzzola who created them at the request of his friend Fr. Slavko Barbarić, a man and priest with a heart of gold. On each of them, except for the one depicting The Garden of Gethsemane, there is an image of Gospa.

Cross Mountain is a place where pilgrims can meet with Jesus in His passion and where they can discover His Love.

On the 24th of November 2001, on the first anniversary of Fr. Slavko Barbarić's death, a memorial in memory of Fr. Slavko was erected in the spot where he surrendered his soul into the hands of the Lord: Fr. Slavko's relief is encrusted in the stone. Situated between two marked Stations of the Cross, it will stand as a sign and a reminder of a man who said what he thought and did what he said, living by the words of the Gospel and the messages of the Queen of Peace.

On the 24th of November 2001, on the first anniversary of Fr. Slavko Barbarić's death, a memorial in memory of Fr. Slavko was erected in the spot where he surrendered his soul into the hands of the Lord: Fr. Slavko's relief is encrusted in the stone. Situated between two marked Stations of the Cross, it will stand as a sign and a reminder of a man who said what he thought and did what he said, living by the words of the Gospel and the messages of the Queen of Peace.

Mother's Village, established in 1993, is an orphanage founded for the education and care of abandoned and neglected children. There is a statue of Fr. Slavko in front of Mother's Village, placed there upon his death. The statue is the work of Italian artist and sculptor Carmelo Puzzola.

The Way of the Cross

STATION I – Jesus is condemned to death

STATION II – Jesus carries His heavy cross

STATION III – Jesus fall under His cross for the first time

STATION IV – Jesus meets His sorrowful Mother

STATION V – Simon of Cyrene help Jesus to carry the cross

STATION VI – Veronica hands Jesus a cloth to wipe His face

STATION VII – Jesus falls under the cross a second time

STATION VIII – Jesus is comforted by the crying woman

STATION IX – Jesus falls under the cross a third time

STATION X – Jesus is stripped and given gall to drink

STATION XI – Jesus is nailed to the cross

STATION XII – Crucified Jesus dies on the cross

STATION XIII – Jesus is taken down from the cross and laid in His Mother's lap

STATION XIV – Jesus is laid in the tomb

Jesus, you have victoriously risen from the dead

The Cross on Cross Mountain

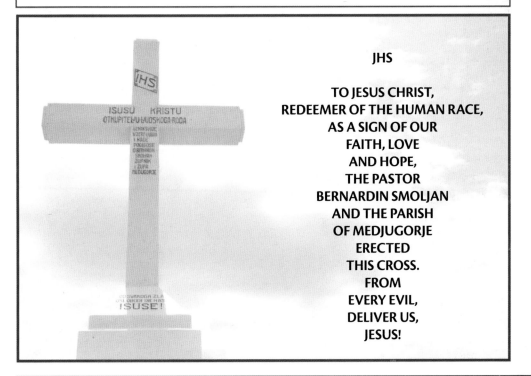

JHS

TO JESUS CHRIST,
REDEEMER OF THE HUMAN RACE,
AS A SIGN OF OUR
FAITH, LOVE
AND HOPE,
THE PASTOR
BERNARDIN SMOLJAN
AND THE PARISH
OF MEDJUGORJE
ERECTED
THIS CROSS.
FROM
EVERY EVIL,
DELIVER US,
JESUS!

,,Dear children,
as I invite you to pray for those who have not come to know God's love, if you were to look into your hearts, you would understand that I am speaking about many of you. With open hearts, sincerely ask yourselves whether you wish for the living God or whether you wish to remove Him and live as you please. Look around yourselves, dear children, and see where the world without God is heading, it wanders in the darkness of temptation. I give to you the light of truth and the Holy Spirit. It is God's plan that I am with you, to help you so that my Son, His cross and His resurrection may triumph in your hearts. As a mother, I desire for and pray for you to unite with my Son and His works.
I am here; decide!
Thank you!"

Gospa was very sorrowful during this occasion.
As She was saying, "I give to you the light of truth and the Holy Spirit"
Mirjana saw a special light glow behind Her
(Apparition to Mirjana on the 2nd of June 2011.)

"Dear children!
Give thanks with me to the Most High for
my presence among you.
My heart is joyful seeing the
love and joy in living my messages.
Many of you have responded,
but I await and seek the sleeping hearts
to awake from the sleep of disbelief. Come
even closer, little children,
to my Immaculate heart so that I may
lead you all toward eternity.
Thank you for having responded
to my call."

A message from the Queen of Peace to the world on June 25, 2011
through visionary Marija Pavlović-Lunetti

Content

Dear Readers, please refer any thought, proposal or suggestion you may have concerning Medjugorje and this book to the following e-mail address: mario_vasilj@yahoo.com.